BIG BACKPACK—LITTLE WORLD

By Donna Morang

ISBN-13: 978-1461146674

ISBN-10: 1461146674

Acknowledgements

I have to give my daughters Brandi Morang and Ginny Loeb full credit for the reason this book began. They asked me to write about my life abroad, so it would be recorded for my grandchildren. Then as it progressed, it became a new and fun adventure for me. I didn't dream of turning it into a published book, but because of you, it became a reality. Thank you both for your continued support of your mom's crazy life.

My students -- without you my life in your countries would have only been seen through the eyes of a tourist. Instead, you made me a part of your lives, and made me feel like a special member of your family. You were my teachers, and you taught me to love your country, as I loved each of you. Muchas gracias --- Cam ong

Friends from around the world -- for sharing part of your life and your incredible stories.

Kathleen Sedgwick -- the first reader of the beginning chapters. You were a positive reinforcement in my continuing with this outrageous endeavor.

Chandra Friendly -- who read my beginning manuscript, and brought structure to my chaos. Joy Eckel for pushing the editing one step farther. The Puerto Vallarta Writers Group for your listening and encouragement. John Ames who read the whole damned thing, carefully watching for errors.

Nidia Veronica Galindo Aldape and Cuauhtli (Pozole) Rivera Ramos, my wonderful and talented ESL students from Puerto Vallarta, Mexico -- for the fabulous book cover and fantastic chapter drawings. You inspired me to take this book to the end and publish your incredible designs.

To my daughters who allowed me to leave home
&
To my students for giving me a new home.

PROLOGUE

How did a woman from Montana, who simply wanted to have some fun and teach English around the world, end up on the border of Thailand and Cambodia, with guns from both countries pointed at her?

That was my question as I kept walking across the long, lonely bridge between these two countries. I wondered if I would ever see my two precious daughters again, or if I'd I be shot and end up floating face down into the big, muddy Kah Bpow river. It was hot and humid, but I knew the sweat pouring off my body wasn't from the heat. It was pure and simple from nerves. Each time I turned to see the guns in front and behind me, I heard myself give out a strange little nervous giggle. I knew the bridge wasn't a mile long, and that it didn't take me hours to cross, but the thoughts that ran through my head were so bizarre I felt as if I were in a Monty Python show.

As I got closer to the Cambodian blockade, the guns looked bigger and the men looked younger. There is nothing like walking toward six smiling young boys pointing big machine guns at you! They all had such cute grins on their faces it made me wonder what they had in mind to do next.

To hell with the guns pointed at me! I was a tough Montana woman, and I'd face them with a smile of my own! And so I kept walking.

How had I gotten to this strange moment in my life?

CHAPTER 1

It was my daughter Brandi's fault. She sent me a magazine, aptly named *Transition Abroad,* published for people interested in traveling and teaching English as a second language. It described what ESL (English as a Second Language) was and listed hundreds of schools around the world. Sitting in my little house in Montana, with snow already on the ground and the fireplace blazing I looked at it and thought "Oh! My God, this is what I have been waiting for all my life!" The phone rang and my daughter asked, "So where are you going, and when do you leave?" I knew at that moment I was going to do this, and with my daughter's blessings. Trembling with excitement, I made a list of things I had to do to put my plan in place.

The truth is, I had never heard of ESL, TEFL, or TESOL (acronyms for teaching English to students of another language) before. While I waited for the school to contact me, I read everything I could find on teaching English as a second language, and I loved everything I read. Now I was more determined than ever. Once I decide to do something, I usually just jump in and give it one hundred percent. And with the help of the Universe, I often succeed.

Having sent my information to New World Teachers, I anxiously awaited their response. Then I would need to pass their aptitude exam and be accepted. So I spent the week on pins and needles.

Wahoo! Pop out the champagne! I passed my exam and was accepted into the ESL teaching program. New World Teachers was expecting me in Puerto Vallarta, Mexico by November 1, 2000.

Everything was happening at a dizzying pace. Every fiber of my being overflowed with excitement. I called everyone I knew and a few I didn't know well at all. It had been years since I had felt this much enthusiasm for life.

Daily, I checked off completed items on my to-do list. The only things left were to attend a few celebration parties and catch a flight to Seattle. After spending a few days with my daughters, I was ready to leave for Mexico.

I had my passport, credit cards, plane ticket, and my backpack was loaded. This was the beginning of a new life of teaching, traveling, and adventure, and I wanted it to start now. I finally talked my daughter Brandi into getting on the road before I went crazy with waiting. At last, I could relax and enjoy these last few moments with her. We were laughing and talking about what an exciting future I had to look forward to when I heard—tires screeching, dirt and gravel flying, and metal ripping. What I saw was an eighteen wheel truck coming directly towards us onto the Seattle I-5 freeway. The noise was deafening, but I'm sure my daughter could still hear me screaming, "Hit the brakes, holy shit, it's going to hit us!" At that moment, I knew it was the end.

Amazingly, this monster truck slowly tipped on one side and skidded across the freeway without touching another car. When the dust cleared my daughter was telling me, "Mom, you'll never get to the airport. It'll take hours to get this truck out of here, it's completely blocking I-5. Grab you pack and run down to the next on-ramp. Maybe someone will give you a ride."

My pack was twice as big as I was, and I had a carry-on, plus a purse. How was I supposed to run down the freeway? "Come on!" she yelled at me. "We can do it! Just hurry before the police get here." She grabbed my little pack and purse, while I shouldered into my big-ass pack, and away we went.

We barely squeezed by the crashed truck on the edge of the freeway, but we both made it down the on-ramp. Cars were whizzing by, but no one stopped to give me a ride. They could see the wreck behind us, so I was sure someone one would stop soon. Sirens and flashing lights were arriving, and a policewoman was yelling at us to "Get back to the car, it is illegal to be standing there, get back to the car now!" I told her I would, but that I was out of breath and needed a minute to rest. Brandi and I decided that I'd stay on the side of the freeway and try to hitch a ride while she ran back to her car. A quick kiss, and away she went. I gathered my packs and purse and crossed the freeway, hoping it would be easier for someone to stop on the other side. Oh, God, more police...As they sped by, they were waving and screaming for me to get off the freeway. Over-head a TV helicopter was filming the wreck. Later I learned I was on the news about a wreck on Seattle's I-5 south bound lane when they mentioned someone trying to hitchhike. The reporter described me as some old hippie loaded down with backpacks running down the freeway.

Some terrific young man, in the oldest, beat-up car I'd ever seen running, stopped for me. He'd seen the wreck and a woman with a heavy load and understood I was trying to catch a flight. He was now my knight in shining armor. He took me all the way to the airport, which was a bit out of his way. He knew I had to be there soon, and that I may never get another ride today. When I offered him money all he said was, "If you had been my mom, I would hope someone would help her. I can't wait to tell her about you, and what you're going to do." I thanked him and dropped a fifty in his ashtray. It had looked like I wouldn't make my flight, but, there I was at the airport, on time and on schedule.

As I hurried into the airport, I saw that mine was the only ticket counter with people lined up, and the line wound all the way around the corner as far as I could see. I asked other people in line what was going on. No one seemed to know; it was just some problem with our airline. After waiting about an hour, there was an announcement; those people flying domestically should come to counter AA-2, those people flying internationally must stay in line, they would get back to us as soon as possible. The only thing the airline told us was their computers were down. Some woman in an airline uniform finally gave us a bottle of water, and a quick smile before vanishing.

Somewhere around the third hour of waiting in line, they announced that international passengers could proceed to counter AA-5.

The local news was broadcasting live what was happening at the airport. For the second time today I was on TV, because they were interviewing passengers in front of me, and I just happened to be caught again. Strange but true, the airline's entire computer system had gone down, all over the world. They couldn't print boarding passes for international flights, so we just had to wait until the problem was solved.

As I waited and waited with nothing to occupy me, my mind went into overdrive. I began to question everything I had planned. What was the Universe handing me? Would it drop me on my head or hold my hand and smile? How could I leave my daughters for several months at a time? What about my little house I had spent the last year restoring? Would the renters destroy all I had worked so hard to renew? What the hell was I going to eat? I didn't even like Mexican food! What would I do about sun-burns? I'm a blue-eyed blonde and burn to a crisp at even a slight hint of a sunny day. *Oh, my God, maybe I should just end all this right now, and call my daughter to come and pick me up. No! I can't do that I'm not a quitter!* Then I laughed at myself and thought, *Isn't it wonderful to feel the burst of adrenaline again, and not know what tomorrow will bring?"*

Finally, after four and a half hours, I cleared security and with a huge smile on my face and a slight pounding of my heart, boarded my flight to Mexico.

It had been one hell of an interesting day, and as I flew away from my old life, I wondered whether I was up to this wild new life. It still seemed a bit crazy, but oh-so exciting for a fifty-something woman who had spent her life in small towns of Montana, Alaska and Washington and had raised her family in rural America to be going abroad to teach English.

Sitting back on my flight to Mexico, I couldn't help but laugh about my old friends' concerns about my plans for a new career. They had always questioned my sanity, from moving to Alaska and taking a baby into the Alaskan bush in the 70s, to buying a farm in Washington when all the farmers were going broke in the 80s. It was a good thing they never heard about living on a boat in the Seattle harbor and painting boats for a living. I wondered what they thought when one day I saw a 110-year-old falling-down shack of a house and bought it. I know I never told any of them about my hunting and fishing adventures, because no one, especially men, want to hear a woman talk about catching huge fish, or hunting bear in the Alaskan wilderness. Yet, they all loved it when I opened an art gallery in Big Timber, Montana, because that was a nice, safe and sane lifestyle. Some of their concerns were justified, as I had done some odd things in my life, but I just love to try new things, and now here I was again.

When I was leaving Montana, my dear friend Larisa gave me my first journal and left the following inscription, which I try to live by.

"If you're not walking on the edge, you're taking up too much space."

CHAPTER 2

I'd come to Puerto Vallarta to take a class in teaching ESL. I had no idea what to expect. At the time, it was just a fun idea I had read about, and it sounded like a good way to travel without being a tourist.

Here I was in Mexico at last, and the first day of school was facing me. I knew where and when classes started, and had been told by the school, to take the bus through what is known as "the tunnel" and what a ride it was! I thought it was going to turn into a crazy story for my daughters to tell: how their mom died on the bus before she even started her first day of school. No one else on the bus seemed to be nervous, but with every wild turn and huge bump, I found myself giggling and grabbing the seat in front of me, preparing for the inevitable crash. Happily, I arrived at school safe, sound, and wide awake. With such an exhilarating way to start the day, I would definitely be alert for the start of class every day.

When I walked in the door and saw the young and eager faces of the other students, I wondered what the hell I was doing there. I was by far the oldest student in the class of twenty; even older than our instructors. I could tell the other students were trying to be polite, but I was sure there were a few snickers about Granny.

Class started with the usual introductions and telling a little about ourselves, where we were from, why we were there, and what we wanted from our ESL teacher training. Then we had a much-needed coffee break, with people breaking off into small groups, and thankfully a couple of the young men joined me. They asked if I wanted to have lunch with them, and it certainly brightened my day, as there were many cute, young girls they could have had lunch with instead.

When we returned from break, our instructors informed us that we would be team teaching an ESL class for local students the next day. There were three of us in each group, and each was to present one part of a lesson plan. Lesson plan... Did we even know how to prepare one? This was dead serious stuff, and I knew I'd better buck up and do a proper job of it, if I didn't want to embarrass my teammates, or myself.

I spent all night preparing for my fifteen minutes of fame. To my surprise, it all went quite well, and I wasn't the worst practice teacher in the class. My students seemed to be happy to have me for their teacher. I learned later that most cultures believe that with age comes knowledge, so they thought I was one smart teacher.

I loved my Mexican students, and I loved teaching them over the next month, but I certainly didn't enjoy the constant observation by my classmates and instructors. Remember how snotty junior-high girls can be? I thought some of the girls in our teacher training class still fit that bill, giving brutal criticism to their fellow teachers. Teaching the students was a walk in the park compared to their critiques.

Each teaching group had taught for fifteen minutes, and then it became thirty minutes. After the second week, we each had a small group of students to teach for an hour while half the teaching class observed and commented. Therefore, I taught every other day, and after approximately fifteen hours of teaching students, I was supposed to be a competent ESL teacher. Unbelievably I felt I succeeded. I cannot envision any teacher walking into a classroom of foreign students that know not a word in English, and try to teach them without some knowledge of the unique teaching techniques that an ESL, TEFL, or a TESOL teaching program offers. These programs all use a similar teaching style, much like teaching a baby to talk.

We had thirty days of class, and then we were supposed to be off teaching in some other foreign country. I can't say I ever gave a lot of thought as to what my next step would be. I just wanted to do well, and receive my diploma. It was all so new and exciting, not just the classes, but to be in Mexico, and be able to think about actually living there, or in any other foreign country. I felt like a teenager again, with the opportunity to do anything I could dream of doing. Once I had that diploma, it would open more doors than I had ever imagined.

Don't think it was all study and no play. I loved going to the Los Muertos pier to watch and talk to the kids fishing there. Walking along the streets in Mexico with the new smells and sights was like living in a movie. I adored drinking tequila or *cerveza* with salt and lime at night with the local people at the bar next to my hotel, listening to their Spanish, and trying to learn a few words every day. Every morning I couldn't wait to get on the bus for my morning giggle, and to see what the day would bring.

Everyone from our school was staying at the same hotel, so it was never dull. Usually someone was having a party, or something entertaining was happening. One night, four Canadian guys who were staying at the same hotel, came home seriously drunk. Living next door, I could hear everything from the barfing to, "Tell me I didn't go to bed with her, please tell me I didn't!" I hadn't seen these boys before, but the next day I recognized the barfing boy's voice. While we were all standing in the hallway, I told him that last night, I had seen him with an exceptionally classy woman. Then I inquired about his health, and hoped he felt better today. All his friends thought it was a whopping good poke at him, and we had a lot of laughs at his expense for the next week.

We became friends and at night, they would come next door to my room where we would pass the tequila and tell our best stories. I guess we were a little loud one night, and the young girl across the hall (she was one of those that forgot to graduate from junior-high) came over to tell us to be quiet. The boys gave her a hard time, and in response, she asked them, "So why are you hanging out with her when you could be hanging out with some of us?" Rod, my barfing friend, told her, "Cause you're a bitch, and she's not!" This started a friendship with these guys that still continues. She however, never seemed to like me after that night.

November 11, 2000 was my fifty-seventh birthday. I woke that morning feeling a little lonely for my daughters and questioning what I was doing, but it didn't last long. Rod, my barfing friend, arrived before breakfast with flowers and balloons and then took me snorkeling for the day.

This was my first time snorkeling, and when I got in the water and put my face under, I had a huge panic attack. Not being a strong swimmer, but loving the ocean, I truly wanted to do this, but how could I with my heart pounding out of my chest and my brain screaming—*get out of here?* Somehow, I got away from the group of swimmers and slowly calmed down enough to try to put my face down again. Once my face was finally in the water, I saw the most amazingly beautiful fish swimming right in front of my face. There were hundreds of little turquoise and yellow ones, striped ones, white ones, and some big enough that I wished I'd brought my fishing pole. I was so involved with looking at the fish that I forgot to be nervous. To overcome my fear for the moment, was the best birthday present I could give myself.

Later that day we went to Mismaloya beach where the famous John Huston movie, "Night of the Iguana," was filmed. It was a very romantic place to walk around, even in the daytime. We swam, ate tacos, and handsome Mexican men serenaded me when they heard it was my birthday. They insisted on toasting me with tequila to the point that I didn't think I'd ever make it up the hill to catch the bus back home. It turned out there was no need to walk when I had four lovely Mexican men, and one Canadian to carry me.

Returning to our hotel, some friends from my class had arranged a party for me with balloons, beer, and tacos. Who would ever have thought I could have such a lovely birthday alone (well not alone) for the first time in a foreign country?

Not everything was a delightful experience. There were times I got lost, or took the wrong bus, or had my credit card stolen. We all hear how we need to be careful about being robbed in foreign countries, and that we should always be alert. I had heard all of this also, and I was careful on the streets. Little did I know I would invite thieves into my hotel room.

My robbers turned out to be *gringos* living in the same hotel as me. This couple used to smoke outside my room in the hallway, and we became acquainted. On their last night in Vallarta, I invited them into my room for a drink. The next morning, as I did every morning, I went to check that I had put my passport and credit card away in their little hiding spot. No credit card! Where could it be? Did I forget to put it away? No, my passport was where it should be. I knew where my card had gone. Those two sweet kids had taken it while I was in the bathroom. I needed my credit card, as I didn't carry cash, and I had to get it canceled before they could use it. All I had to do was call the 1-800 number, and I would be okay. First though I had to find a telephone that I could use. No, I couldn't use the telephone at the front desk and the office wouldn't be open for an hour. I knocked on the door of the bar next-door, and the nice owner let me use her phone. How can I call the credit card company when my card is gone, and I don't know their 1-800 number for lost cards? This was not as easy as the credit card companies made it sound, at least not when you're outside the U.S. I had no idea how to reach them, and so I called my daughter. After several calls, she was able to cancel my card and have a new one issued. Thankfully, my little thieves hadn't used it. I'm not sure I learned a lesson, but I did learn to hide all my important goodies in better spots. I now write down all telephone numbers, and passport information, and keep it in a notebook which I hope no one would ever thinks to steal.

Late one night the desk clerk at the hotel was pounding on my door, telling me to hurry because there was an emergency telephone call for me. This was not good, because in my family, the only emergency call is if someone is dead or dying. I tried to hurry, but I honestly didn't want to answer that call. When I finally got to the phone and found my voice there was a strange person yelling, "Don't hang up, please don't hang up! Those stupid bastards keep hanging up! Please go find Donald, he's on the third floor." I was so happy that it wasn't about my daughters, I quickly ran all the way up to the third floor to get Donald. What Donald's emergency was I never knew, but he didn't seem too concerned when I told him he had a call downstairs. I understood the desk clerk making the mistake between Donna, my name, and Donald, the man on the third floor. After that burst of adrenalin, going back to sleep wasn't going to happen for awhile. Thankfully, I had a new Grisham novel to keep me company.

Thanksgiving was the last day of class, and our school planned a turkey dinner and graduation ceremony for us. We were all anxiously awaiting the presentation of our diplomas, and recommendations. Yes, I received my diploma and a great letter of recommendation! But best of all, was my daughter Brandi arriving to spend a few days with me. It was such fun to show her all my favorite places, and teach her to drink tequila like the locals, with a twist of lime and a lick of salt. We snorkeled, fished off the pier, went to Mismaloya beach, and she met some of my students. I know we danced on the bar… maybe several bars, not sure if we "shot out the lights" but I do know we laughed a lot.

I made a decision to start my journey going south. After one month in Puerto Vallarta, I had a diploma in ESL, a good letter of recommendation, and a feeling of immense accomplishment. So with my backpack loaded, I caught the bus to Zihuatanejo.

CHAPTER 3

With Puerto Vallarta in the rear-view mirror, I was on my way to Zihuatanejo, Guerrero, Mexico. I didn't care that they said it was a twelve-hour bus trip; I was so excited it could have been a twenty-four hour trip, and I'd still want to do it.

When I got on the bus at 4AM they said it was a twelve-hour trip, but, I now know it was much closer to fifteen hours of winding roads and speeds to make Mario Andretti (a very young Mario, because our driver appeared to be about fourteen or fifteen years old) seem like the slowest driver in Mexico. For the first two hours of the fifteen hours, I sat with my legs and arms braced for the inevitable crash. This bus, and the crazy winding road that hugged the side of the mountain reminded me of two best friends who had drunk too much tequila, with its unending curves and head banging bumps. Once the sun came up it was a little more relaxing as the scenery was so spectacular; palm trees on one side and the ocean directly below at the foot of the cliffs to the right. Even if this was my first and last bus trip in Mexico, there was nothing I could do except sit back, and enjoy the view.

Finally, we stopped for lunch, high on a cliff at a little roadside restaurant. Everyone on the bus jumped off and hurried inside; while I jumped down, and took the time to look at the amazing view and have a cigarette. By the time I got inside, everyone had the most wonderful looking shrimp soup I had ever seen. I asked the bus driver what it was called, and he told me it was "*sopa de camarón*." So I asked the server for a bowl of s*opa de camarón* and the *Señora* shook her head and told me "*no mas*." So I asked for the "*tamales con pollo*," but again she shook her head and replied " *no mas*." This went down the entire menu. Finally, I asked for a ham and cheese sandwich, and she nodded her head and said, "*Si, pero no tengo jamon*" (Ok, but we don't have any ham). It just goes to show that if those damn cigarettes didn't kill me, they sure ruined a good meal.

Somehow we all survived our ride and arrived in Zihuatanejo. Struggling with my Spanish dictionary in the taxi I finally managed to tell the driver where I wanted to go. I found a room at Hotel Suzy, which was only about a half-block to the beach. It was a nice little hotel, and my room had a balcony looking out at a lovely private garden with beautiful and strange flowers, or at least strange to someone who has only lived in frigid Montana, frozen Alaska, and icy-cold Eastern Washington. I was intrigued by not only the beauty but also the size of some of the plants I had only seen as houseplants in the US.

The first and most important thing on my to-do list was to check out the beach. Just to the left of Hotel Suzy was a nice restaurant called the Arcadia. I stopped for a cold *cerveza* and watched the Mexican children swimming in what didn't look like great, clean water, but it must be okay, or they wouldn't be swimming in it, right?

So excited-- I jumped in, and very shortly I had an excruciating pain in my foot. I didn't want to scream, but it just came out of my mouth. I couldn't really see anything on my foot, but man oh man, did it hurt! An old Mexican fisherman nearby, raced over and started rubbing sand on my foot. Knowing only a few words in Spanish; nevertheless I understood his body language, and it was saying, "*vamonos!*" I hobbled back to the Arcadia, where all the waiters were waiting for me. They seemed to know what was wrong. One of them pulled up a chair, grabbed my leg and told me, "Keep it up above your head, way up above your head!"

Only a few minutes had passed since the sting/bite happened, but already I could see a red line quickly going up my leg. I knew this wasn't good. One of the waiters, known as Big Johnny, got a good hold of my ankle, took out his pocketknife, and quickly slashed open the bottom of my foot. He squeezed it until a fair amount of blood was flowing, grabbed a lime and some salt, and rubbed the lime on the cut... and then this horrid, nasty, vicious, sadistic man, poured salt on it. You have heard the expression "adding salt to the wound!" I now know the true meaning. My God, the pain! It was as bad as the fish bite.

By now, we had acquired quite a crowd, and I was about as embarrassed as I could be. The good thing was I saw the red line disappearing. By now all the waiters were having a lot of fun with my foot, massaging my legs, and discussing what fine legs they were. Ok guys, even I know when enough is enough! The crowd that had gathered was now getting bored, and perhaps a little disappointed that I was going to live after all. No one ever told me if the fish-bite could have killed me, made me sick, or what. I was just happy to have the red line disappear.

One nice thing did come from that awful stinging fish. I made some fun new friends and found a great place to sit and enjoy the view. In all the hours, I spent at the Arcadia I never did see another foolish person go swimming in that part of the bay. The children still swam close by, but I noticed they never went into the area where I was stung by that nasty fish.

Usually I started my day at Playa Madera for a few hours of great waves, nice people, and sun. Later I'd go back to the Arcadia for a *cerveza* and to visit with the waiters. One day I mentioned to them that I'd loved to go fishing, but I thought the charter-boats were too expensive for my wallet. Being good men, they understood a fellow fisherman, and arranged for me to go out with one of their friends who had a *panga* (small boat). Paco, the *panga* captain, met me for lunch, and we set up a time and a price for my first fishing adventure in Mexico. Luckily, I found another gringo who wanted to go along and would share the cost. Paco picked us up at Playa Principal at 6 AM, and immediately he set up our poles, and we started fishing as soon as we left the beach. Within minutes, Marty and I both had a fish on. Paco laughed at our excitement because these were only small bait fish, but it was still exciting to us.

As we entered the open ocean, we saw two magnificent sailfish jumping and playing right in front of our boat. Paco told us we wouldn't go after these as they were just too happy, and we'd have a better chance a little farther out. Seeing those sailfish jumping free and playing was one of the most beautiful sights I had ever seen in nature. They certainly made me question why I wanted to catch one. However, being a fisherwoman, I felt a deep desire to hook one of those amazingly beautiful creatures.

The ocean was perfect, and life was good. We were all sharing a beer and having a smoke when; Shuuum—my line went zinging, and Paco yelled, "Fish on!" We all jumped down, and Paco grabbed the pole to set the hook. He was yelling for me to get in the chair and get ready. I was ready! I'd been ready my whole life for this moment. Paco was screaming at Marty, "Reel in, reel in." He quickly handed my rod to me, and I thought for a second it was going to be jerked out of my hand. At that very moment, the fish took a run, and I saw him burst out of the water twisting and turning. Then he made a deep dive, and I was sure I was going to lose him.

Paco kept yelling, "Keep your tip up and let him run! You're doing great, keep your tip up! He'll get tired in a minute. Don't try horsing him in, keep your tip up!" My heart was pounding, and my hands were shaking, and I couldn't really listen to him. I just kept my eyes on my line and where the fish was. My only thought was that this was the toughest fighting fish I'd ever had the privilege of meeting. I had fought some huge salmon before, but nothing like this monster-fish. He seemed to be getting a little tired of the constant pull of my line, and I was finally able to reel him in a little closer. I'd lift my pole, and then rapidly reel as I dropped it down, lift and drop and reel like crazy. What I had gained, he would quickly take back with his next run to escape. After several attempts, he seemed to give up and I got him a little closer to the boat. When he got a look at the boat he gave his best effort to escape, and I watched as this beauty jumped and spun in the air again. I was stunned by his strength and the vivid colors of brilliant blue, deep purple, and metallic silver as he lunged on the end of my line. My heart was pounding so hard I thought I might have a heart attack. Paco was laughing and telling me, "As fast as you're getting him in, it's just a little one." As I brought it up to the boat, I looked at it and thought, *This looks huge to me, it must be at least eight feet long! And look at how long its bill is! I don't care what Paco thinks, this is a monster-fish to me.* I had finally tired him out and brought him in for Paco to release. He looked down and shook his head, and told me he was sorry, but it was hooked too deep for it to survive. As he pulled it into the boat, he grinned at me, shook my hand, and said, "It's not too small." He knew exactly how big it was, as soon as it was hooked, and had been teasing me all along about the size. When we got back to the dock, later that day, he was bragging about the big one his boat caught.

Later in the day, Marty also hooked a sailfish, but Paco gunned the motor at the wrong time by accident, and Marty's fish was gone. We both caught a couple of Mahi Mahi, which were beautiful and also good little fighters. I gave my sailfish to Paco to sell, and to feed his family. The Mahi Mahi, I took to the Arcadia Restaurant where they cooked it three different ways, each one more delicious than the last. I quickly changed my mind about not liking to eat fish or at least the fresh fish caught in Mexico and cooked by fantastic chefs. Marty, myself, and all the waiters were well fed that night by my first fish from the lovely waters of Mexico.

My new friends at the Arcadia asked if my day had been what I expected and if everything was okay. I had to tell them the truth, if I'd had a heart attack and died from the thrill of fighting that sailfish, I would have died one happy woman!

I had come to Zihua to find a job teaching English, so I thought it was about time I tried to find one. I asked everyone's advice on where I might find a teaching job. It didn't sound as if there were many options, maybe only three or four language schools, one of them being a children's bilingual school and the other two ESL schools; one of which taught several languages, and one a regular ESL school for all ages.

It was a Monday, and I had my resume, diploma, and letter of recommendations in hand. At all the schools, I heard the same answer; they didn't have anything now, but maybe later.

I continued with my daily beach routine, and enjoying the people of Mexico. I tried to practice my Spanish, but everyone wanted to practice his or her English. I didn't think I was improving very quickly, but I sure loved helping them with their English.

One night I was at a restaurant, and I heard two waiters arguing over which one would get to serve me. No, it wasn't because they thought I would leave a big *propina* (tip), or because I was so beautiful, they wanted me to help them with their English. I think it was really dawning on me as to how important my teaching could be for people to improve their lives. Until now, I had just been thinking about myself and how cool it was to have a way to travel and make a little money. I must have missed the importance of this in our class, or perhaps they neglected to impress on us how our teaching could be a life-changing chance for our students, and the entire community.

After only a couple of weeks in Zihua, I felt right at home. Since it was a small town, everyone knew I was an English teacher looking for a job, and they were all trying to help me. Then it just happened out of the blue. I was walking down the street, and Donilo the owner of Everest school, yelled across the street to me, "Hey, teacher, can you teach tomorrow?" I had left my resume with him a few days before so I at least knew who he was. I thought this was a strange way to get a job, but I'd take it any way I could get it.

Later I met him at his school, and he wanted me to teach three classes starting right then. Ok, this was a little crazy, but by the time I had worked for Donilo for almost a year, I realized this was not strange for him to go out on the street and yell, "Do you want a job? Can you start teaching right now?"

Donilo is one unusual man. He is a genius, and holds three degrees from Yale, but he can never button his shirt right. He is a deep-sea-diver that works on boat engines, under water, yet he is afraid of and hates the water. When I asked him why he did this, his explanation was that he wanted to be an engineer, and he was afraid of water, so he wanted to overcome his fear. However, he hasn't, and he doesn't think he ever will.

I asked Donilo to write me a letter of recommendation when I was leaving. He told me "just write it yourself, and I'll sign it because I can't do a very good job saying what I want in a letter." Yes, he is a genius. Hell, maybe he just bought all those diplomas, which could very easily happen in Mexico.

I was lucky enough to know and spend time with most of Donilo's family. Often I was invited to his restaurant, which his elderly Mother ran for him. One night we celebrated Donilo's father's one-hundredth birthday. For his Father's birthday, Donilo gave him a cane. Not the least bit happy with the gift, the old man hit him with it and told him to take it home, as he wasn't in need of a cane, or maybe Donilo could use it himself, but get the damn thing out of here! This one-hundred-year-old man was a terrible flirt, and he would always wink at me when his wife's back was turned, and call me his *pequeña rubia* (his little blonde). Aw those Mexican men, even at one hundred they never quit flirting.

My very good friend Rogelio, who was a waiter at the Arcadia, had a *gringo* friend with a car. So thanks to Rogelio's friend Chad we had Saturday or Sunday outings to the countryside. Rogelio wanted to take us to his Grandmother's farm, and we planned to take a picnic, pick up his Grandma and go to a nearby beach. Grandma's farm was about 30 minutes from Zihua. It was just a wonderful little place with flowers everywhere, bananas, papayas, mangoes, chickens, and a couple of her neighbor's pigs. The pigs were the first order of the day; to get them back home and out of Grandma's yard. Poor Grandma had been chasing them all morning. Rogelio told me that I was a big hit with his Grandma because I chased the pigs back home, and she didn't think a *gringa* would ever do that.

In the afternoon, we loaded the car with anyone around. Young kids, old people, and even a baby. It was a treat for them to get to leave the farm for the day. This wasn't a beach that tourists went to, but an out of the way little place that the locals kept as a nice secret.

Rogelio's son, nine-year-old Oscar, and I spent most of the day trying to catch crabs with our hands, but we weren't very successful. I'm not sure what I would have done if I had been lucky or unlucky enough to have grabbed one of them. Just like all crab they do have pinchers, and they will use them. Oscar and I had a good laugh when we looked up, and found we were both covered in mud. Laughing, he smeared more mud on my face, and told me, "Now you look like a Mexican!"

Rogelio later told me, "Oscar never likes women, because he's afraid I will marry them, and he wants me to go back with his mother. But he told me you could come to the beach with us again because you played with him all day, and you didn't kiss me once." (What he didn't see won't hurt him.)

Oscar and I spent quite a bit of time together and got along very well. However, when I would try to get him to speak English, he became a little brat. He told me he liked my funny Spanish, but hated it when I spoke English with his dad. He never did learn English, and I still speak funny Spanish, and we are still friends.

During our day at the beach, a family from Mexico City arrived with two little girls and their mama. They hadn't ever been to the beach before and were scared to death of the water. They could see their friends across the river coming into the beach, and they wanted to join them, but had no idea how to get across the river. While their friends across the river were yelling for them to wade across, the little girls started to cry. Rogelio understood what was happening, and told them we would help them. So he and I carried the little girls across to their friends. My little girl had a death grip on my neck, and I just kept patting her on the back, talking, and telling her my name. My Spanish was so limited I didn't know what she was saying. I just wanted her to feel okay and safe with me. Think about how scary it would be if a strange person from a different country picked you up and carried you across a river, which you were already afraid of. Later in the day we heard, "Donna, Donna, Rogelio, Rogelio!" The little girls wanted us to come take them back across the river. I felt at that moment, as if I could walk on water or just fly them across, I felt that happy.

The people from Mexico City are known as *Chilangos*. Apparently, it is thought in Mexico that the *Chilangos* don't like *gringos,* and that the people in other cities of Mexico don't like the *Chilangos*. It is possible on that day we crossed those boundaries and two little girls may be the ones to change those feelings in the future.

The use of the word *Chilango* is similar to *Gringo*; it can be used as just a term for where you are from, or it can be used derogatorily, depending on the tone or facial expression.

The next Saturday we were invited back to Rogelio's Grandma's for lunch. When we arrived, Grandma wasn't anywhere around. While we were waiting for her to return, Rogelio decided to climb a papaya tree and pick us fruit for lunch. He yelled, "Donna, come catch it!" Oh, okay. Down rains the papaya, and while grabbing for the fruit, I broke one finger and sprained another.

Oh, God, the pain! I don't even like papaya, so why did I do this? I guess because someone needed help, but more likely, it had to do with the fact that I live my life in the moment. At that moment, a papaya was coming down, so I was there to try to catch it.

A couple of days later I was at the Marina Café, a very American restaurant, enjoying great barbecued ribs, baked potato, and salad with blue cheese dressing. I had been eating nothing but tacos for over a month, and I'd been told that this was a fantastic and cheap restaurant. Plus it had a book exchange. There was a Gringo sitting next to me and he asked, "So, how's your finger?"

Laughingly I asked him, "So, how do you know about my finger?"

With a smirky smile, he replied, "Oh, everyone in town knows about your foot that the fish bit, your finger, your new teaching job, and we think you're either from Montana or Alaska. Hey, it's a small town, and you're the new kid around town."

I didn't ask, but I did wonder what else they knew about me. Having lived most of my life in small towns I understood what he was saying. I guess I thought that it would be different living in a foreign country. I may have been even a little flattered that they were interested enough to discuss me.

Oh, I forgot that I'm teaching and not just playing. I can't use the word working, because it was too much fun, to be labeled as work.

Everest English School had a great location on Nicolas Bravo, one of the main streets. It wasn't anything fancy, but it had nice large rooms with modern white-boards, and adequate books. The rooms were quiet so when someone was teaching in the next room you didn't hear them, except occasionally if the students become excited over something.

On Tuesday through Thursday I had about a dozen students. On Monday and Friday, the class size was reduced to about six or eight students, which seemed to be the standard for all teachers.

Most students in Mexico seemed to take an extra day off each week from class. When I asked students about this, I received many answers. One of the reasons I received is "my grandmother died" one student's grandmother died every week. When I asked how many grandmothers he had and how they could die every week, he told me he just couldn't tell me he wanted to go to the beach, or he wanted to sleep, but that is just the way we are in Mexico. One student told me he couldn't come to school because his pig died. That became the school's joke: if you didn't want to do something, "my pig died."

Every single day was too rewarding to get upset with someone choosing to come to class only four days a week. I quickly learned that life in Mexico wasn't as serious as in the USA, and to accept the differences. My students were paying for their classes, and it was their choice to attend or not. My goal was for them to love their classes so much that they didn't want to go to the beach or sleep late. I wanted my students to improve their English, but also to instill in them how important their own country is. I used a lot of Mexican history in my classes for conversation and reading. Being new to both teaching and Mexico I was a little gung-ho, but my students seemed to become more interested each week in learning English.

A teacher in Mexico is highly respected, as is an older person, so I had a lot of respect coming my way. I was told that what a teacher says is more important than what a parent says, so I was careful in what I told my students. My students weren't just sitting in silence waiting for me to shower them with gems of wisdom. They were interactive, and at times, everyone was talking at once; definitely a cacophony of sound.

I wasn't concerned about perfect grammar I just wanted them to speak, as long as it was in English. Yes, there were times when it all went south, and I heard a lot of Spanish, but a quick reminder of "English only" and they quickly got back on track. Most of the students really were interested in learning. Occasionally a student was there because their parents demanded it. Nevertheless, these students could be fun and made for an interesting class. Surprisingly, it was other students who became upset by a disruptive student.

I did have two boys who really didn't want to be in class and would sit outside behind a car and smoke. I knew they had come to school but weren't coming into the classroom, and I knew where they smoked. So one day before class, I took my cigarettes and joined them. They were shocked and a little embarrassed, but when we finished our smoke, they came to class with me. As we entered the classroom, all the kids were laughing and told us, "You stink like stinky cigarettes, and you'll probably die! But Teacher, you got these guys to come to class."

In my very first class, I had a mother and son; the son was a new-age kid with purple hair, baggy pants, a big attitude, and wasn't the slightest bit interested in learning English, which made me feel like a complete failure. Watching the lack of interest in his eyes, I told them the story about the strange fish that had stung me. This boy, who had acted like he never heard a word I said, jumped up, grabbed a marker and started drawing the fish, and explained to me that this horrid fish lies in the mud, has a spike on its back and shoots poison at whatever it touches. He thought I was very brave not to have cried or gone to the doctor. It was a good learning experience for me because just when I felt like I was failing him, he responded and rebuilt my confidence.

I guess it was imperative to find the right switch to click on his interest, even if it took a painful episode to do it. This boy and his mother became my best students and good friends.

Lesson 33--- Keep trying, even if it's painful

CHAPTER 4

I'd only been teaching at Everest School for a few weeks when Donilo wanted me to open a new school in San Jeronimito, a *pueblo* (village or small town) 35 minutes by bus from Zihuatanejo. I decided to think it over, and go see what the little *pueblo* had to offer. At first look, it appeared to be a sad, rather dirty, and extremely poverty ridden little village. But immediately I knew I wanted to stay and do what I could to help these people. I was a little unsure of what I was getting myself into, but it felt good as I told him, "Yes, let's do it." Donilo just sat grinning at me said, "I was sure you'd want to do this, so I made all the arrangements for it to happen right away."

He had rented a nice building for the school, and then we went to see the room he had also rented for me. Ok, it wasn't the Ritz, but I thought it would be just fine. The owners were very loving, and they swore to Donilo that they would watch over me. My room had a very, very bad bed with springs popping up, and I wondered how my poor old body would fit around the bumps. It did have an acceptable bathroom. This was to be my new home; a bad bed, a fan, and a bathroom.

Maria the owner, had purchased a camp stove and a cooler, so I would have a way to cook in the room next door. It was quite crude, but I thought I already loved the sweetness, and the simplicity.

Maybe it was Maria and Joe that made it all look so interesting. But it was more what I thought teaching in a foreign country would be, than teaching in a resort town, with all the comforts of home.

My little *pueblo* had one highway running through, and one other paved street everything else was dirt roads, so San Jernomito was a bit dusty at its best. It had a lovely park where the people gathered in the evenings for volleyball, to meet friends, or take romantic walks. It also had a small open market, where I found great tacos or a yummy breakfast. It may be a little *pueblo*, but there wasn't anything I needed that I couldn't buy there.

My school—and I do mean my school, (as Donilo had given me full rein) had a small problem. We had no students. That was the first thing I had to do, find students. My assistant Abraham and I went through-out town recruiting students. It wasn't difficult to cover the entire town in one day, walking and talking to everyone. Abraham told me, "Everyone in town knows what we are doing and who you are. They are all happy that you came here to help us." We were hitting the streets to recruit students when the mayor stopped us, and wanted us to know that his daughter, wife and friends would be signing up for classes. He told us he would do everything he could to help our school and that he was very glad to meet me. It looked promising for the school, but these people had no money, which was the biggest problem. Donilo, Abraham, and I discussed the money problem, and my thoughts were if we could make enough money for my rent the first month we would be doing okay. We all agreed the most imperative thing was to help the people of San Jeronimito, not to make money. We decided to wait until after the New Year, to open for classes. Therefore, I planned to spend the holidays back in Zihua.

The boys at the Arcadia restaurant in Zihua had made bets on how long I would stay in San Jernomito. One of the waiter was from there, and he had only given the odds of my staying; no more than two days. He told the others, "There are no other *gringos* in town, and why would a single woman want to live in a place like that?" Rogelio had given me the longest, but that was only one month. I was still thinking it was going to be a great adventure for me, and a wonderful opportunity for this little pueblo, to make a better life for everyone. Knowing about the bet also made me want to show them what a tough and determined *gringa* I was. They had always seen me dressed for school, or the beach and they all agreed, "she is just too lady-like or she's some kind of a little princess." There isn't an English translation for what they thought about me. Little did they know how far I'd go to win a bet, or to prove them wrong!

I was happy to return to Zihuatanejo, and wait until after Christmas to make the move to San Jeronimito. The holiday events wouldn't have been the same without my Zihua friends. Ramon one of the waiters at the Arcadia, invited me to a celebration. His daughter was turning fifteen, and in Mexico this is an important celebration called the *Quinceañera*. Traditionally, when a young girl turns fifteen, she goes from being a *nina* (child) to a *señorita* (woman). The *Quinceañera* begins with a religious ceremony. Later, friends and family are invited to attend a fiesta where the young girl and friends perform what is called a "Court of Honor." The young girl and her "court" of friends or relatives do an intricate dance. The *Quinceañera* wears a white gown, and her *damas* (attendants) wear colorful, long, fancy gowns, and the male *chambelanes* wear tuxedos. The dance I saw was so well choreographed it was hard to believe they were only fifteen years old.

First, a favorite relative presented Brenda, the young girl, with a glass of champagne and then she and her court drank a toast. Next, her younger sister presented her with a gift. The grand finale was the tradition of the "Changing of the Shoes" where her father removed her flat shoes, and placed high heels on her feet, to signify her coming of age. This was incredibly touching, and definitely a tearjerker.

The tables were all decorated with flowers and candles, but also supplied with bottles of rum, Coke, and ice. Later we all had a fantastic Mexican dinner of tamales, enchiladas, tortas, rice, beans, and everything you could imagine for a Mexican celebration. After this lovely dinner, everyone danced until dawn. Before I left, Brenda presented me with a gift as a thank you for dancing at her *Quinceañera*. I felt extremely privileged to have been invited to such a personal and beautiful celebration.

Someone later explained that this is lovely, but at times a sad tradition, because the parents often go into great debt to provide their daughter with an elegant *Quinceañera*. I later heard stories of people even selling their homes to have this celebration for their daughters.

It was suddenly Christmas Eve, and this was my first time without my daughters at Christmas. I thought I was doing fine until I called, and heard their voices. Then the tears came, and I spent most of the conversation crying. I can't say I was lonely, I guess it was just their lovely voices that brought on this emotional downpour. As I was talking, or more accurately crying into the phone in the hotel lobby, a friend walked by, and told me to meet him at the Arcadia, and to quit crying, or I might worry my kids. So that is what I did.

There were many familiar faces at the Arcadia, and the sadness of hearing those sweet voices and missing my daughters was forgotten. A couple of *gringo* friends asked if I wanted to join them for Christmas dinner, and I quickly agreed.

So the next day, we met and went shopping for our Christmas dinner. We all agreed turkey was out of the question as we could buy lobster for about the same as what a turkey would cost. Each of us picked out our favorite food, and then went back to Chad's house to prepare our gourmet feast. I cooked lobster and fish-cakes, Chad prepared steak with mushrooms and asparagus, Big Dave did caviar and smoked tuna, and our new friend Tracy from Oregon who had spent the night with me because she couldn't find a room in the whole damned town, did an elegant salad and fantastic shrimp. It was truly a *gringo fiesta* with lots of *cerveza*, tequila, and *vino*. It wasn't a bad Christmas for being my first away from my daughters.

Christmas is of course the high season for both American and Mexican tourists in Mexico, so all the hotels and restaurants were full. My friends at the Arcadia had warned me that if I wanted to be there for New Year's Eve I should come early to get a table. But Rogelio told me not to worry, as I had been invited to Jimmy's table for the big party.

Jimmy and his crew had arrived in Zihua a few days earlier, and I happened to have had a table at the Arcadia when they arrived, and I do mean "arrived." Jimmy was a big shot bull rider from New Mexico and owned a bar in Troncones, a small village north of

Zihua. Everyone at the Arciadia knew Jimmy, and said he was one rich, bad guy. The only reason they sat with me was because there was no other table; but Bridget, Jimmy's girlfriend at the moment, took a liking to me and Barry, Jimmy's best buddy and I quickly became friends.

What a showstopper Jimmy, Barry and a former Miss Texas (Bridget) were when they drove up to the Arcadia. Miss Texas would stop traffic anywhere in the world, as she was so gorgeous. She also had new fake boobs, which she was very proud of, and would tell you the story of how she got them, or show them to you if you asked. However, the real attraction for the local people was in the back of Jimmy's rig; two beautiful brand-new Harleys. Jimmy was also driving a new Ford truck with a crew-cab, which was pretty impressive anywhere in Mexico, but Zihua was one hell of a long way from the Texas border. Not everyone could get this far into Mexico and still have two Harleys in the back of a new Ford truck. Not being anyone's dummy about Mexico, Jimmy also had another truck following him with his security guards. He never went anywhere without his body-guards. His guards were huge Mexican men and no one would think of messing with Jimmy or anyone near Jimmy, under their watch.

Now I have to tell you that Jimmy was really one bad dude. I have known some bad-ass guys, and Jimmy was number one. So what was a nice old lady, who didn't do drugs, doing with this crew? I'm not sure how it all happened. I guess Bridget wanted another woman around, and Barry liked my sense of humor. Jimmy didn't care if I existed or not. However, if you think I was going to turn down huge platters of lobster and shrimp with shooters of tequila every time they arrived, you are crazy. No one is that bad to dine and laugh with.

I spent New Years Eve with this group of rowdy people, plus Rogelio, and it was one first-class party. We were wined and dined on lobster, shrimp, buckets of champagne, and mariachi bands played all night, especially for us. This party was all thanks to Jimmy.

Later someone built a bonfire on the beach, and while we sat by the fire, Mexican singers serenaded us. We bought little wooden boats from a young beach boy and he had candles to light the boats as they sailed away to the New Year. This is a Mexican tradition for those living on the beach. We also wrote a message, something from the past we wanted to get rid of, threw the message into the bonfire, and burned up our past. This was a tradition from some other foreign country. It was a new and lovely way to enter the New Year.

About a week after our New Year's Eve party, I saw Jimmy and he had two black eyes and a terrible cut on his arm. When I asked what bull ate his lunch, he was eager to tell his story. It seems, he and Barry had a race with the new Harleys and Jimmy went through a barbed-wire fence and over a cliff, totally destroying his bike; and Barry, being a good friend, followed him over the cliff. So now, they had no Harleys until new ones arrived from the States.

The cut on his arm was infected, and he now had a bright red line going up his arm, which he knew wasn't good, but it did get him a lot of attention. His friend Barry was concerned and nagging Jimmy to go to the doctor, but Jimmy was still making light of it. Finally, he sent one of his bodyguards to the pharmacy to get him some penicillin, and right there in the restaurant he sat and gave himself a shot of penicillin, and then had a shot of tequila to go with it. It didn't work though because later he came close to dying from that infection.

While everyone around him was eating lobster, steak or whatever they wanted, Jimmy ate habanera salad, that is habanera chilies with hot sauce on it. You could smell the heat of it, but he didn't even break a sweat. I was never sure if he loved them, or just loved the attention he got for eating such a thing.

My friend Bridget was getting a little jealous as Jimmy had a new girlfriend. Alma was a Mexican girl from a small pueblo in the mountains, but she was not your local naughty Mexican girl. She was one sweet and innocent girl, and no one knew how Jimmy found her or what was happening with them.

Two weeks later Jimmy and Alma were engaged and making wedding plans. Shock of all shocks, Jimmy was not drinking or partaking in any of his drug abusing normal activities. Bridget was going back to Texas, and Barry was thinking that the world as he knew it had gone crazy. The waiter's tips at the Arcadia had certainly diminished with the lack of Jimmy's lavish parties. I sort of missed all the lobster I could eat, but the truth is they all lived in the fast lane, and I was aware that they were all big trouble. We would all go back to living a more normal life, and poor Alma; I only wished her great success with her future husband.

Jimmy, Alma and Barry all moved to Troncones, a little spot on the beach north of Zihua, and we didn't see any of them around town very often. We heard many stories that Jimmy was taking over the town, and the people of Troncones were not happy about him living there. They were sure he was running drugs and girls, and wanted him out of their quiet little *pueblo*. Jimmy had built a huge and elegant house in Troncones, and then he started a feud with his new neighbor. The report in the local paper was something like this. It seems that Jimmy and Barry had threatened to kill their neighbor, and nightly had been shooting at his house. They were arrested, but released, and were then accused by the neighbor of giving bribes to the police (like that is something new in Mexico). The feud went on; with shots fired from both sides until the neighbor finally gave up and moved.

One night while I was at the Arcadia Jimmy and Alma quietly arrived. They weren't near as flashy as in the past. The waiters did their duty, but the mood had changed. Barry, later arrived and we had a laugh or two, then he told me he had to attend to Jimmy's needs and that was the last I saw of them.

Jimmy and Alma supposedly bought a hotel in Acapulco and left Troncones the following year. Sad to say, my sweet friend Barry died of an over-dose of drugs. I never heard from Bridget, but I bet she's still having fun.

CHAPTER 5

My new year didn't start off that great. First thing in the morning, the ATM ate my credit card. Of course, the banks were all closed, and so I had no money. Not being sure what to do about the eaten credit card and no money, I went in search of Donilo. He assured me not to worry as he knew the bank manager, but we would have to wait until Monday when they unlock the machine. It wasn't all that easy, but without Donilo, I don't think I would have ever gotten my card back; they would have just returned it to the U.S. bank. I did learn that you only have five seconds to pull your card out before it is sucked back into the machine. It was important to get your card out before you retrieve your money. I knew I would never do that dumb trick again. Meanwhile, Donilo gave me enough money to get by, so everything was okay and back to normal.

After Donilo and I returned with my credit card in hand and some pesos, we made plans for him to pick me up at my hotel. January 2, 2001, was the big day for the move to San Jeronimito. This trip was for real, and I had to admit I was a little nervous. I had only been teaching for a few weeks, and my Spanish was almost nonexistent. What did I think I had to offer this little pueblo? As soon as we arrived, Joe and Maria were there to greet us, and I felt everything would work out. How could it not be good when everyone wants you to succeed?

Maria was so concerned about my comfort, that she had brought a cooler full of fresh fruit and vegetables for me. My room was freshly painted, everything was clean, and as charming as it could be. I knew they were worried that it wasn't fancy enough for the new teacher (I sort of over heard this conversation). It really was nice enough for me, and I told them not to worry that I was a country-girl, and I liked a simple life.

I loved our courtyard where Joe had flowers planted everywhere, and the first thing I did was ask if I could help take care of the garden. We agreed I could do the watering and some weeding, so Joe could relax. I knew they felt better when he showed me where the hose was for watering the garden, and we talked about how often to water, and how he liked his garden to look..

The first night that I was out watering the flowers a little burro walked into the garden, and nudged me out of the way. As he munched all the weed, and none of the flowers, I thought this might be the answer to easy gardening. I also had a mama pig and eight babies that came through every night. Yes, animals do just roam the streets freely, and somehow go home at night. I loved my little pigs' nightly visit, and occasionally they even ventured into my room. Truth be told, I immediately loved it here, except for my horrid bed.

The next day Abraham met me at my new home, and we went around town to check on our students whom we thought we had enrolled. Then we checked on how the school looked, and if everything was ready. We still didn't have the school up and running after a week of crazy things like the electric bill, which the former tenants hadn't paid, and now we had to pay before the electricity would be turned-on. Books hadn't arrived, and the desks or tables hadn't been built. Our (my) school is just one fair sized room so painting should only take half-a-day, but two days later it still wasn't finished. Maybe tomorrow it will all be completed. *Mañana*, is an important word to know in Spanish because everything will happen tomorrow. *Paciencia* is also required, and I was slowly becoming a bit more patient.

Classes finally started, and I had a total of twenty-four students enrolled. Classes were held from 8-10AM and 4-6PM. All the students were pretty much at beginner level except for one student, Tony, and he was fluent in English, having lived in the US for several years. Tony and Abraham were my paid assistants, or should I call them my lifesavers. These two young men were my translators, do everything that needed to be done men.

If you had been able to visit my class, these are some of the students you would have met:

David was a taxi driver in Zihua. His first day he didn't speak any English, but after one week, he knew how to make a proper introduction, colors, and body parts. We also did special work for his job of what I called "taxi talk." His goal was to be able to speak English well enough to drive a taxi in Ixtapa, a resort town, and that required sixty percent speaking English. He did this after one month of school with his dedicated work. In addition, I gave David private lessons, so he was able to progress faster than most.

Tania was a real pistol. She talked and talked, but she would just say any old word she knew. It was never correct, but she kept us all laughing. She was a Jehovah's Witness, and yet wore the lowest-cut blouses, and more make-up than the hookers in Zihua. I was never sure if she was allowed in church looking the way she did, but that was how she dressed for school.

Adrienne told me she couldn't come at 5PM and wanted to come at 7PM instead, because she watched television at 5PM. You had to love her for her honesty. This was one of the biggest problems for scheduling classes. They wanted to come when the time was right for them, not on someone else's schedule.

Celestine was an old-fashioned Mexican girl. She dressed in the older traditional style, with a long colorful skirt, and a gathered top of mismatched fabric. She was a soft spoken and shy young girl, and English didn't come easy for her. She wanted to be able to move her family to a bigger city and get a job working with tourists. We worked not only on English, but also on a stronger voice and direct eye contact.

Esquila, who I called Tequila, was an engineer. He paid for six months of school, and bought books for all the students, markers for me, and then he told me he couldn't come to class very often, maybe only today and tomorrow. That was the last I saw of him. I guess he just wanted to help the school, and his community.

Tony, my lifesaver told me he was going back to LA in a few weeks. I knew I would miss him, in fact, I wondered how I would do classes without him. Tony went to Ixtapa every night to drink, and dance with the tourist girls. He told us, all the girls loved his face and they thought he was European. On his last day of class, he told me, "I think that when you were twenty-one, you must have had a lot of fun, and drove the men crazy. Now you are old, and you are still fun, you laugh a lot, and I don't think you are afraid of anything. I think I love you." Well, is that just the greatest thing to hear from a twenty something young man, and you're a fifty something woman.

One day before Tony left for the US, an elderly Mexican man wandered into my classroom, thinking it was where he had to go to pay his electric bill. When he saw me standing in front of a group of young Mexicans, he stopped and stood glaring at me, and then he spit on the floor and uttered a string of nasty words. Tony gently took his arm and led him out of the room. Everyone was quiet, and I knew my students were nervous and a little afraid, and they knew I was embarrassed and uncomfortable, but no one mentioned the man. In a few minutes, Tony and the old man returned. Tony told us in English and Spanish that the man was very sorry, but it had made him angry seeing a *gringa* speaking English with his Mexican children. Tony explained to him that I was helping everyone in San Jeronimito, and teaching them English. Still this man was angry, he explained that he had lived in the U.S. for twenty years, and no one had ever helped him learn English. We listened to this man voice his anger, and then I decided it was time to try to take control of a sad situation. I was a little nervous, but I put my arm around him, and told him he could come to my class, free, and we would all help him learn English. I saw his anger disappear, and when he looked at me he had tears in his eyes, and kept saying "*lo siento, lo siento*" (I'm sorry, I'm sorry). We all tried to convince him to stay for a lesson, but I think he was just a little ashamed and too embarrassed. Tony explained that the old man couldn't come to class because he lived in the hills behind town, and it was way too far to walk everyday.

I was glad that Tony had been there for this uncomfortable situation and had done a beautiful job of taking good care of everyone involved. I had wondered if there were people that didn't approve of a *gringa* teaching English in their community. I wasn't foolish enough to think that everyone would welcome me with open arms. Of course, there should be people questioning who this person that had arrived in their village was, and what was she doing with their children? I was just content to be welcomed as graciously as I had been.

I loved my classes and living in San Jeronimito, but it certainly wasn't an easy life for the local people. I felt a deep need to help this little village in any way I could, and become just a regular part of their community. I hoped that soon the local people wouldn't even notice when I walked down the dusty streets, or ate at the market, but at that time I still drew a lot of attention.

Everyone was excited when I ate at the market with them, and someone always paid for my lunch. We all laughed a lot at my Spanish, but they tried to help me, and I would teach them a few words of English in return. I loved the food at the market, and the fellowship of the local people; the only problem was that they closed at 4PM, when everyone usually ate their main meal, and I wanted and needed food at night.

My students told me to go eat at the "Chicken Ladies" so nightly I went in search of her. I found taco man, pizza kids, and corn people and finally, ah ha, I found the chicken lady. She had a little barbeque grill on her porch, and she was happy to see me almost every night. She told me I was eating too much *pollo* (chicken) and no *verduras* (vegetables), "it is bad," so she started cooking a vegetable every day for me. Maria also invited me to dinner at least once a week, and she was an amazing cook. I was getting fatter, but certainly having fun finding my night time meals.

I didn't have a refrigerator in my room, but I did have a cooler, so every couple of days I needed to make an ice run. There were only two places in town I knew of to get ice, and I had my favorite place. Every time I went there, the lady would yell to her husband, "Come, come, the beautiful lady is here." I'm not sure if anyone ever told me I was beautiful before, so of course I bought my ice from her; in fact, if I wasn't having a great day I'd go just to hear her yell those words to her husband.

I had made a few trips to the local hardware store, and the man who owned it and I became friends. I would ask for what I needed in Spanish (using my dictionary before I went) then repeated it in English. I would write it for him, and then we would practice his new words. One day as I was walking back from class he drove by with another man. They stopped, and he introduced me as his teacher. He was so pleased to tell his friend, I was his teacher. It made me once again aware of how proud these people were to learn even a little English.

I washed my clothes in the *lavadera*, which is a cement sink with a corrugated bottom, rather like having a giant, old fashioned washboard. This was a standard item in all the courtyards, and it made me feel part of the real Mexico. Maria and I shared the clothesline in the courtyard, along with the burro and a few pigs.

I learned to live without a fridge, and that eggs sitting on the shelf instead of a fridge were ok. I still had a hard time seeing mayonnaise sitting in the sun, but people didn't seem to get sick from it. I was trying to work my way up to it, but it just seemed something to stay away from, at least for now. I'd gotten used to the cold showers that filled the bathroom with water. In fact, I'd come to enjoy the cold water, and thought all showers would be better not enclosed. When your shower was finished, you had also cleaned the bath-room.

At night, I practiced my Spanish, read, or went to watch the activities at the park. There was always something going on at the park so if I was bored, that was my entertainment. Normally, there was a volleyball or soccer game, and at times, little kids practiced riding a bike or learned to skate. The park was where everyone went at night, and it was a charming spot with courts for basketball, volleyball, and lovely trees and flowers everywhere. Every morning when I walked through the park on my way to school, I wondered why there was so much garbage. I talked to my class about doing a community project and installing big garbage cans in the park. They all listened politely, and then Tony said, "That's a nice idea, but what about the ladies who clean the park every day? If we do this, they won't have anything to do, and they will lose their jobs. Plus someone would steal the barrels." I decided that some things were better left alone. When I walked through the park, I knew it would be a mess in the morning, but by noon, it would be clean once again. Most important, I knew the ladies would still have a good job, and that is the way it should be.

Every Sunday morning I heard roosters, lots and lots of roosters. I saw people carrying them in small cages, and I thought they must be going to the market on Sunday.

Joe told me, "No, they're going to the cockfight. They hold a big cockfight just down the street. Do you want to go?"

I had never been to a cockfight before so I said, "Yes, let's go."

He politely told me, "There won't be many women there because it's a man thing, but I will tell them the *Maestra* (female teacher) wants to see it, and it will be ok."

I'm not sure what I thought it would be like, but it was all quite interesting. We sat waiting for the handlers to prepare their fighting cocks properly, and then it was a very fast battle with one cock the winner. The preparation of each bird took several minutes. The cocks were first fitted with their spurs, and this looked quite technical, as at times the handlers tied and re-tied the spurs until they were satisfied with the fit. Then the roosters were carried into the ring, and the handlers would shove the birds at each other, but still holding them. Once the birds were angry, they were thrown at each other, and within one to two minutes one of the birds was usually dead. I think the basis of all of this is not so much the cockfight, but the sport of betting. After a couple of fights, I asked Joe, "How do I place a bet?" Everyone around wanted to take my money, so that wasn't a problem. I bet 100 pesos the first bet, and I won. Then I bet 50 pesos with the same man, and I won again. Now everyone was laughing and talking about the *gringa maestra* and how she was winning every bet. Joe was so proud of me, and telling everyone that I was a farm girl, and I knew my roosters. That was the last bet I won, but for a short time the local men were impressed with my choice of birds.

Cockfights are one of those illegal things in Mexico, but are still a popular sport in many villages. I know I had fun, and didn't find it near as offensive as the bullfights that everyone else seemed to enjoy.

After being away from home for a few months, I think my daughters were getting a little lonesome or curious about where I lived, and what I was doing in Mexico. It was so exciting as they both decided to come visit me. My Friend Joe took me to the airport to pick them up, and I had dressed in all my fancy Mexican style clothes, which we all had a good laugh about. My new duds were soft gauzy material and a bit lower cut than I usually wore. So they had their moment of poking a little fun at Mom. Then we returned to San Jeronimito, so they could see where I lived, visit my school and all my new friends. I'm not sure who was more surprised by their visit—the girls and where I lived, or the people of San Jeronimito that the *Maestra's* daughters had come to visit her. I know everyone in town turned out to look at the two beautiful girls with long blonde hair; a pretty strange sight in that little town.

After one night in my lumpy bed in San Jeronimito that was enough for them. Plus, I wanted them to see Zihua, so I could introduce my daughters to all my friends there. It was such fun to show off my daughters, and to show the girls my wonderful new home. After only a short visit, they both had to return to work, which broke the hearts of many men in Zihua. It was a little lonesome for me without them there too.

Joe and Maria were the best thing that could happen to any person in a new town. They introduced me to everyone, showed me the local area, and kept me well fed. They had made my living there so easy and so very lovely.

Maria was a citizen of the U.S. and spent twenty-five years in LA, but only spoke a bit of broken English. Joe was an incredible man. When he was only fourteen years old, he left San Jeronimito and walked all the way to the United States. At that time, there wasn't even a road from San Jeronimito to Zihuatanejo, it was still an unclaimed jungle. This incredible adventure took him more than four years, but he did it. He traveled to every state in the U.S. except Alaska and Hawaii. Joe speaks perfect English, and told me that after arriving in California, his goal was to get to Chicago, and after one more year of doing whatever he had to do, he arrived there. His first job was at a lumberyard. His boss told him if he couldn't name all the lumber in English in one week, he'd fire him. So he learned, and never quit learning. Everyone knows Joe, and we laughed that no one had ever called him Jose, but he is well known as Joe or American Joe.

Maria, had always dreamed of opening a restaurant, and had decided it was the proper time to put her dream to the test. We talked about what she was going to serve, about her hours, and who was going to help her. She asked if I would like to help her make tamales.

As I watched Maria mix the *masa* and lard together for the base of her tamales, with her big spoon and hands, I thought how much easier it would be with a mixer. I also knew I was watching the authentic way it was done by women in Mexico. The smells were intoxicating from her concoction of peppers heating on the stove. Maria had already soaked the chili and removed the seeds, so I wouldn't have to do this part of the job. She explained it was a chore no one liked, because if you rubbed your face or eye, it burned like the devil. She gave me the job of shredding the meat and then adding it to the chili sauce. I also soaked and prepared the corn husks for the beginning of my tamale journey.

Maria patiently showed me how to spread the *masa* on the corn husk, with the back of a tablespoon. Then add a little of the meat and chili mixture. Next came the most difficult part, for me, of folding the husk and tying the ends into a nice looking package.

Two days and a hundred tamales later, I'm sure poor Maria was sorry she'd asked me to help her. On my side of the kitchen counter where I'd worked was a total tamale mess, and across the kitchen counter where she'd worked there was not a sign of tamale preparation. I had tamale juice in every crevice of my body, and my clothes were completely covered with sauce. There were globs of maize stuck to my chair, and I knew I'd ruined several corn husks, to the point they couldn't be used. Maria never lost her smile, and we continually laughed and talked, her in her broken English, and me in my broken Spanish.

I had a delightful time, and by the end, my tamales looked almost as perfect as Maria's; but the first fifty, I think the family had to eat. Opening night of the restaurant was quite successful, as everyone loved Maria's cooking. However, people did complain that it was a little too expensive. My God, it was three tamales for 10 pesos or about $1USD! I thought with all the work it took, they should have been one tamale for ten dollars.

Sad to say but Maria's restaurant was only open for a month, and then she became too sick to keep operating it. Maria's health, a strange heart problem, was always a concern for Joe, yet he never stopped her from her desire to open a restaurant. Her food was fantastic, and her *pozole* was the best I've ever eaten. In Mexico, we would call Maria's *pozole, "muy rico"* (very rich, or very tasty). Maria heard this from many customers, and I often saw her turn her back and smile. This is the nicest complement you can give to a cook in Mexico.

One other day Maria invited me to go with her to a baby shower. I didn't know the woman, but Maria insisted that I would be welcome, and the woman would be extremely honored if I came. There was music, dancing, lots of goodies to eat, and more to drink than any of us should ever consume. All the women took turns asking me to dance, and were excited that I was having so much fun with them. We ate, drank, danced, and laughed like crazy. I'm surprised the pregnant lady didn't have her baby that night. It was by far the most fun I have ever had at any baby shower.

Later that same night, I heard lots of laughter and noise outside my window, then a knocking on my door, and the music began. Four young men had come to serenade me. Not being sure what to do I sort of peeked out the window. About that time, Joe charged out of his house, and yelled, "Get the hell away from my house, or you'll have buck-shot in your butts!" The boys took off running, but one of them fell and broke the vases Joe had along the walkway. Everyone was yelling and laughing, and I thought it was hilarious, and so sweet. We never found out who the boys were, but the next day the news was all over town, and everyone was laughing about the Saturday night serenade -- except Joe.

Abraham, my right hand man at school, invited me to lunch with his family, so we could all meet. Abraham had told me that his Grandmother was eighty-six years old, and made tamales and *atole* (a drink made from corn) every day. She woke up at 4AM to prepare her food, and then loaded it onto the bus to Ixtapa. She carried her tamales and *atole* on and off the bus all by herself. This little lady stood in the hot sun all day, selling her wares to the local workers. When she wasn't cooking or selling her food, she worked in the orchard and the fields with the rest of the family. I was shocked to meet this tiny little lady, at eighty-six, she still looked younger than me, and was as sharp as a tack.

We had a delicious lunch of chicken, rice, beans, and lots of different kinds of fruit from their orchard. When I asked Abraham why we didn't have his Grandmother's tamales, they all laughed, and he told me, "This is a special meal for the *Maestra*, not street food for the workers." And indeed it was a special meal.

Abraham's family was extremely proud that he had such a respectable job, and worked for an American teacher. His mother told me, "Abraham almost died a couple of years ago from rheumatic fever, and we didn't believed he would be alive to do such wonderful things." Abraham was in his twenties, and had never had a girlfriend, but now he was ready because he had the respect of his family, and the community. He was a great young man, and it was my honor to work with him. I hope he got a nice girlfriend as he deserved one--- or more.

Easter is the most celebrated holiday in Mexico, and we had a long vacation as all the schools in Mexico were closed for at least two weeks, and some for the entire month. We could have closed, but didn't; and only a couple of people came to class the week before we finally closed for the holiday.

Zihuatanejo was packed with people from all over Mexico, since this was the time to travel, visit family, and go to the beach. I was lucky to have a friend to stay with because there were no hotel rooms available. I had a terrific vacation, seeing friends, going to the beach, meeting new people and hanging out at my favorite spots.

If you lived in Zihua and wanted to have fun you went to the Jungle bar, but if you wanted to hangout with the local people you went to the Corner bar, and that is where I went many afternoons. One afternoon while I was there I met Pedro, a Zihuatanejo teacher, and he told me, "I have to shake your hand. I have heard much about you, the teacher from San Jeronimito. Many people talk about the blonde American teacher helping the poor people from the *pueblo*, and now I have met her." Well, my heart felt like singing, I was so proud that he had heard of me, and that I was respected for my actions. In return, I was also pleased to meet Pedro, because I had heard that he was the best Spanish teacher in Zihua. We had a couple of beers together, and talked about teaching in Mexico, and what an impact it had on the entire community.

That same day I met another Donna at the Corner bar. We shared a beer or two, and then Pedro returned to ask me, how long Donna and I had been friends?

I told him, "We just met"

He laughed and said, "I thought you guys were old-time friends the way you talk to each other. But, I wondered why a teacher was such good friends with a prostitute."

Donna smartly told him, "I don't care that she's a teacher, if she doesn't care that I'm a prostitute." We became good friends, and the local people seem to think this was very nice of both of us. She may be a prostitute, but to me is she is a friend and a lady, whom I'm happy to know.

During our long Easter holiday, my daughter Brandi returned to see more of Mexico with me, and we took a trip to Mexico City. Being a bit foolish, we took the bus instead of flying. It can be a rather enjoyable trip, or a trip from hell! It depends on what class of bus service you purchase, or happen to receive. We did book first class, and going to Mexico City was lovely, but still an eight hour trip on a bus. The trip home was a different story.

Everyone will tell you if you are going to go to Mexico City, go during *Semana Santa* (Easter week) because everyone from there leaves town and goes to the beach. The traffic was still outrageous, and I found Mexico City to be just an enormous and formidable city. It was difficult to find a decent hotel or even an open restaurant, but we had come here to see the pyramids, not to see the city.

Neither of us had ever seen pyramids before, and Teotihuacan is simply astonishing. Climbing to the top of the Pyramid of the Sun was almost as scary as jumping out of an airplane, and almost as high (it's 248 steps, and higher than a 21-story building). I'm so glad I did it because I will never do it again. I remember my daughter charging ahead and telling me, "Come on Mom you can do it." Once

I finally got to the top, I took a breather and sat down on the top step. Next to me a young girl suddenly stood up, and walked down the stairs as if it was a normal thing to do. As I watched her, my first thought was, she was committing suicide, and my heart beat even faster. When I finally stood up I thought I might pass out, but I gathered myself up and clung to the sides of the wall. My daughter was shocked as I really used to jump out of airplanes, and now I couldn't even enjoy the height of the pyramids without feeling queasy. Instead of walking down the steps, I scooted my butt down the stairs most of the way. I loved the pyramids much more, after I was back on the ground.

The entire area was just an incredible experience. I thought that these people had to have been an amazing culture, and it was a very emotional experience for both my daughter and me. I'm not sure what took place for me, but once on the ground the tears wouldn't quit flowing. I felt such an attachment to these lost people or something unknown to me. I have felt this same reaction at all the ruins and pyramids I've visited since then. I love them but find that extreme sadness overwhelms me when I'm there. Maybe in 2012 I will find the answer, as that is when the Mayan calendar ends.

Our return bus trip back to Zihua was the worst in the world. It was like sitting in the toilet with smells so strong, we could hardly stand it. I don't think our bus had any shocks, and every bump sent us banging our heads on the roof. This was not the nice, clean, comfortable, first class service, we had going to Mexico City, that was for sure. Even though that was what our tickets read. It also took three hours longer because they didn't use the toll-roads, but wound through the countryside on little side roads. As we climbed out of that nasty bus, we were happy we were back in Zihua.

My daughter's vacation was over, and she left for Seattle. Now I had to decide: whether to stay or leave. Like usual I was thinking of making another jump into a change of life, simply for the excitement of seeing something new.

Before Easter vacation, Donilo and I had talked about closing the school, and having the students attend his school in Zihua, because it just wasn't making any money for him or me. At least we had gotten these students to want to learn English, and they would all continue with their education in Zihua. I had prepared my students for this transition, and they liked the idea of traveling to Zihua daily for classes. They thought the short thirty minute bus ride would be fun, and it was something they could all afford, plus they wanted to go to the big city to study. I hadn't promised them that I would stay and remain their teacher. They all understood how I loved to travel, so they had an idea that I would leave if not now, then soon.

After another meeting with Danilo, we made the final decision to move our students to Zihua. Having made the decision to leave Mexico, there were things that I had to do. I stopped at the airport, to see when I could get a flight to Seattle. The man at the Alaska Air counter told me, "You'll have to go today or wait two weeks." I told him to book my ticket, but that I had to return to San Jeronimito, pack everything, and then get back there all in three hours. He wished me luck, and I hurried out the door. I couldn't believe my good fortune as my student, David was sitting in his taxi right in front of the airport. We raced back to pick up my clothes, and to tell Joe and Maria goodbye. I thought I'd make it, but I had no time to spare. I ran into the airport, and the same man was behind the counter yelling and waving his arms, "Bravo, bravo, Donna. You made it!" Only in Mexico, would a ticket agent remember your name, and care if you made your flight or not.

Then I looked over and there stood Joe's brother, and his nephew who had come to tell me good-bye. I was so overcome I started to cry, and Joe's little nephew was crying and hugging me and asking me to please not go. I don't think anyone had ever made me feel that loved as those people did on that day. I certainly questioned what I was doing leaving this little village and the lovely people. But, I wanted to see more of this world, and so I boarded my flight.

CHAPTER 6

I had been in Mexico for six months, and so "I thought" I could speak basic Spanish, which should qualify me to get by in Spain. With my ESL certificate, a letter of recommendation, and my Lonely Planet guide book, I was ready to discover Spain.

I was a little nervous about Madrid. It's a huge city, and I had read and re-read my travel book on how to get around this city. Despite all the reading, I still felt unsure of where to go and how to get there.

I did know I had to take the subway (the Metro). I had never even seen a subway before, and I was supposed to catch one at the far end of the airport. I had a few butterflies in my stomach. However, after flying for 26 hours, I was anxious to begin my European experience, which I had missed when I was twenty.

Thankfully, I had enough sense to stop and use my ATM card to get some *pesetas*, (Spain's currency) as the subway only accepted *pesetas*. When I stopped again to study my travel guide, a young man stopped beside me and asked, "Where do you want to go?" He was traveling on the Metro also, and as we waited for the train, he advised me on where to get off, and what hotels were the best choices in the main backpacker's area. Away we went, crammed into Madrid's Metro. The poor people around me must have hated that obnoxious backpack taking up so much room and knocking them around whenever I moved.

The first thing that surprised me was the amount of young people necking in public, not that I'm opposed to kissing, but they were all making-out like crazy. I was totally unprepared for this public display of affection! Later, I thought that the kissing in public was one of the sweetest things about Spain, and its people. When my angel from Spain told me it was time to get off, I hated to leave him. He was young, intelligent, interesting, spoke fantastic English, and was my security blanket, for the moment.

But, a lovely surprise was in store as I climbed the stairs out of the subway; another young man asked if he could carry my pack for me. I had read not to let anyone ever take your pack, or to accept help from someone who seems too eager to help. However, it is just not my nature to distrust people, and besides he was so cute and sweet. He took my pack and asked, where I was going. Where was I going? That was a valid question! I asked his advice, and he told me, "Just sit down, have a cold drink, and wait for me." After only a short time, he arrived back with a woman, and she told me to come with her, she had a lovely room for me at her hostel. I suppose this could have been a significant screw-up on my part to go off with a stranger, but it wasn't, and those people were the nicest in all of Spain.

At the hostel, getting to my fifth floor room could be compared to climbing a small mountain. My monster backpack, filled with heavy, heavy books had already become a hated object. I kicked myself for thinking I had to bring so many books. Since this was my first trip to Europe, I had no idea that I could have purchased English books in Spain or found a good book exchange.

After several stops, trying to catch my breath on the dreaded stairs, I thought I'd just stay in my room for the rest of my life once I got there. But after a little *siesta*, I gained my spirits back, and ventured out to see Madrid. The nice lady at my hostel told me where to catch a city tour bus that stopped wherever you wanted. This was a super deal because I could get on and off all day.

After deciding what to do first, I knew I had to see the famous Museo del Prado. I stood in a long, long line, in the beastly heat, but it was worth the wait and the heat! It was amazing to see over 2,000 paintings by such masters as Goya, El Greco and many more. Yes, it was incredible, and I felt like I was such a worldly traveler, not a little country girl from Montana. But, I have to say I loved just riding the tour bus, seeing Madrid's streets, and the people almost as much as the famous Prado, so maybe I'm still a country bumpkin.

The night before I left Seattle, my daughter Ginny made paella for me, and this was the one food of Spain, I wanted to know. I ate paella in every city I visited, and Ginny's definitely won the contest for the best paella. Eating in Spain was not as easy as in Mexico where there were taco stands on every street corner. I usually ended up at a bar with *tapas* (Spanish appetizers, or snacks) that you just pointed to under a counter, and they warmed it up while you waited in line. I was confused by Spain's choice of hard French bread as their standard, as this isn't France. So why the French bread? I missed my tortillas from Mexico.

Whenever I went to a sidewalk bar everyone had a small bowl of olives, and so I would ask for, "*Oliva, aceituna,* olives, *aceituna, por favor.*" I even looked it up in my dictionary, and pointed to the word; never, never did I get my olives. Why? I think in Spain, they don't recognize Mexican Spanish as Spanish. Finally, I just spoke English, and had better luck communicating, except for my olives. It became a challenge for me to win my bowl of olives. No, not ever did I win, but I sat at tables with people and their olives. As I told my sad olive story, someone would usually let me have the entire bowl to myself. And they were oh so good! Unlike any olives, I had ever eaten.

I hadn't planned to stay in Madrid as I wanted to find a teaching job on the coast, after reading that trusty old travel book, I thought that Cadiz sounded like a nice place to start. I told the lovely lady at the hostel my plans to leave in the morning, and asked her about city buses to the main bus station for Cadiz. She was quite upset, and told me "No, no you can't take a bus with your back-pack. You have to take a taxi, or you will be robbed!" So I loaded up that horrid pack, and grabbed a cab to the bus station not quite knowing where I'd end up.

Spain is a beautiful country, and it reminded me of Montana, with its rolling hills, wheat fields, and mountains in the background. I loved the countryside, and every few miles in the distance, an artist had constructed a towering metal bull. These bulls stood about 40 square feet, and there were 97 of them scattered throughout Spain's countryside. It was said that the people of Spain loved them, but the government was trying to ban them, though no one seemed to know why. What a great artistic endeavor this was, and I particularly liked them because in the past, I had done design work for a metal artist.

It took about eight hours from Madrid to Cadiz, but I thought that the buses in Spain were better than flying. I arrived in Cadiz at 9PM, making it a bit difficult to find a room. I'd met a man from Cadiz on the bus, and he had given me some hotel names to call, which made it much easier. He even stood by the phone, in case I needed help. It can be a real problem to use a phone in a foreign country; the money, numbers, and the operators can make a person want to cry. With this charming man's help, I found a hotel in the city center, aptly named "Old Town."

Cadiz is the oldest city in Spain, and it is absolutely beautiful. So decidedly different from any city I had ever seen. The streets were like little winding alleys, and I would get lost so many times a day it was crazy. Sometimes I knew I was walking in circles, but I didn't know how to get back to where I wanted to go. At times, it was exhausting and frustrating, but usually I thought it was just an interesting adventure. There were small parks everywhere, and pigeons by the hundreds, just like in the movies. It was spring, and the trees and flowers were in bloom, couples strolled hand in hand, kids played, and I could sit for hours and drink my coffee, and just observe it all. Or wander the streets looking for a restaurant.

I never thought I had a hang-up about food, but I truly had a hard time getting adequate quantities of food in Spain. For breakfast, I went in search of an egg, which is not difficult. Right? I finally found a place with omelets on their menu, and I was so excited and hungry. I got my itty-bitty omelet, and a hard french roll with a tiny cube of butter. After inhaling the omelet, I went to pay for my meal. They charged $1.00USD for the roll and $1.00USD for the butter. So the next morning, I told the waiter, I didn't want the bread and butter, just the omelet. He brought it anyway, and I told him, "No gracias" again they charged me for it. Okay, they win; I'd feed the bread to the birds, or try to eat this hunk of rock. Sadly, I was still hungry. Daily, I searched for another restaurant serving what I thought was a standard breakfast, perhaps ham and eggs, bacon and eggs, anything filling for my grumbling stomach.

Early one morning the lady from the hotel's front desk knocked on my door and told me, "The hotel is closing, there is a family emergency, and you have to leave, and please leave now." I hurriedly packed, knowing there would be at least a dozen people searching for different living accommodations. I grabbed the first vacant room only a block from the old hotel. I felt rather lucky to have secured a room in the area I was familiar with. Stupidly, I took the room, sight unseen.

My new room barely qualified as a closet, 4x7 feet and a horrid dirty cot for a bed. The walls were just sheets of plywood—this was definitely not the Ritz! At night, my neighbors had sex all night. Yes, it truly went on all night. Even with a pillow over my head, I could hear them. The next morning, I thought I had to see who these people were, so I took my coffee and sat outside our door in the courtyard. When they finally came out, I laughed and laughed because each of them must have weighted 200-300 pounds, and they were not young, just loud. I found a different room later that morning!!

One afternoon I went to New Cadiz, which was just a short distance from the old city, but what a crazy transition from the oldest city in Spain to one of the newest. There were no cobblestone streets or quaint shops, just new, glitzy high-rise buildings. It was rather a disappointment. It was supposed to have a great beach, which I found packed with local (or loco) sunbathers. It was extremely chilly, which warranted my wearing a sweater. I didn't know how they could brave those brisk winds with only a bathing-suit. I couldn't imagine how packed this beach must get in the summer.

Seeing a block-long line of people waiting to get into somewhere, my curiosity was aroused. To my extreme disappointment, I saw the golden arch of a new McDonald. Next to it on the beach was a darling little plaza with seafood restaurants surrounding it, and not one soul eating there. I was truly the only person with probably twenty-five waiters looking at me while they waited for the surge of business. At last, I had a delicious, large meal, and I was fully satisfied for the first time since arriving in Spain. I was quite sure my bowl of steaming clams beat a Big Mac.

I have to admit that I missed Madrid where the people were friendly, while here the only people who talked to me wanted to bum cigarettes or money, and no one ever smiled. I did meet a very nice, happy man from Cuba, who felt the same about the people of Cadiz. We had a jolly good laugh about their not recognizing his Spanish as Spanish, and acting as if they couldn't understand a word he said.

I decided one morning after I ate another crappy little omelet that I needed to find happier people. I had never felt so alone, even when I was by myself in the wilderness of Alaska. I packed my belongings, and at the bus station I decided to go wherever the next bus was going.

The first bus leaving was going south to Malaga, which had to be better than Cadiz, or so I hoped. I studied my travel book, and thought it would be a pregnant idea to stop off in Gibraltar, and cross the Strait to Morocco. When the bus stopped in Gibraltar, I got my pack, and the English-speaking bus driver wanted to know what I was doing. I told him, I was going to get off, and go to Morocco.

"No! You can't go there by yourself that's just crazy." As incessant as he was, I still thought it would be ok.

A young backpacker got on the bus while I was talking to the bus driver, and sternly told me, "Lady, you can't go over there alone. You'll be robbed, raped, and killed the first day."

I hated not to do what I wanted, and I don't usually listen to what other people think. They were both so insistent that I had to give it another thought, plus I needed to let someone know where I was going. I decided to listen to them, and if I chose to I could always come back at a later time. I was sure they would agree to let me off at Marbella, as it was supposed to be a new and classy city.

Wow, Marbella was easy. I just got off the bus, walked down the hill, and found an elegant hostel (elegant compared to what I had been staying in). While waiting for my room, I discovered a nice, clean little café to have a beer, and also a sumptuous dinner of paella. Yes, this was all getting much better.

My bed was so nice and clean, there were no more bed bugs and dirt, no people having loud sex next door, and I thought this was close to heaven. I even had a clean, hot shower to use. Sometimes, we take those little things for granted and forget to appreciate them.

I needed to see this lovely city, so I took off for the beach about twenty blocks away. It was so beautiful; the plazas all had Salvador Dali statues, which were shockingly gorgeous. The trees, flowers, and small parks along the sidewalk were clean and carefully tended. Wonderful elegant shops, art galleries, and intimate restaurants graced every street. It must have taken me half the day to go twenty blocks, because I was in such awe of this gorgeous place. I knew I had found somewhere other than Madrid to love in Spain.

The beach was fantastic with white sand and blue water, just like every picture of the Mediterranean I had ever seen. A little surprised; all the women, young and old, were topless. I was somewhat uncomfortable at first, but then I saw a very elderly lady facing everyone while removing her blouse, and the look on her face was like she was in heaven. After that, I felt as if I were honoring their custom, and so-- off came my top too.

The next day I had two appointments for job interviews. The first school was definitely to my liking, and we discussed pay and hours. It sounded like a perfect fit. Then he dropped the bomb: were my working papers in order? "What working papers" was my answer? Yes, at most schools in Spain you need legal working papers from the government. It looked like I wouldn't be working in Spain or at least not at a legitimate school. He was such a genial man, and told me not to worry I'd be able to get a suitable job in September or October, with good pay at a respectable school, but not now, as the government was watching. I guess I'll just become a beach bum here or go back to Mexico.

One of the best parts of traveling and staying in hostels is the intriguing people you meet along the way. My fellow backpackers have always been much younger than me. Many were European, Canadian, and several Australians. In my travels, I found a huge difference in age barriers that seem so normal in the United States. Whether in class or on the road, my age was accepted and often times honored. Unlike in the U.S. where age seems to be a huge stigma, the backpackers from around the world, invited my presence. I witnessed this in many of my classes also. The older students would sit and chat with younger kids, and it was just a normal thing for them. I found this to be one of those beautiful lessons from traveling. And now once again I had young, interesting, fun-loving roommates at my nice, clean hostel in lovely Marbella. Oh, how sweet it was to find happy, smiling people in a beautiful city.

Laura was from Australia, and this girl had the craziest hair I had ever seen; pink, spiked, and parts of it shaved and other areas long and wild, people everywhere stopped to look at her. She had dozens of tattoos and was still so cute you wouldn't believe it. She was a recovering hard drug user of ten years, and was now so clean she squeaked; no meat, didn't wear leather and was a pure vegan. Laura started her day with running for three hours to the top of the mountain a few miles out of town. In a couple of months, she was meeting her father for a marathon in Singapore. One evening she described her terrible life growing up, her abuse as a child, and then her hard core drug use as a teen. She wanted to know what I thought of her now? I thought this young lady was one of the most incredible people I had ever met, and I would be proud to have her for a daughter. She just amazed me with her survival of life and her complete honesty. I nicknamed her Tiramisu, because she was sweet, but also because the Italian male tourists liked her a lot.

Christy was from Toronto, but now worked in London for the United Nations. She was half Jamaican and half Irish. She had worked for the UN in Indonesia, and had gotten kicked out of the country with ten other UN workers for participating in a political protest. Three of these people had been killed, and two were never heard from again. She was forced at gunpoint onto an airplane in the middle of the night, taken to Malaysia and released. Indonesia charged them with inciting political unrest, but the charges were later dropped, and Indonesia apologized to Great Britain. However, Indonesia still won't allow Christy to enter their country. All she had to say about this was, "It was a bit unnerving, at best." We talked a lot about racial issues in both the U.S. and Britain, and she had certainly experienced her share of prejudice directed at her. She felt this was all just a spiritual journey, with her being a young student.

Kim was from the U.S. but insisted she would not spend her life there, because of her distaste for American politics. It was amusing to hear her talk about George Bush and her political views. She had been studying at the University of Spain. Her degree was political science, and she was well educated in Spain's political history, and also U.S. history. She was a tiny little girl with such a lot of gusto. When she was only fifteen, she and a classmate traveled to Oaxaca, Mexico by train. Next to her on the train a man was stabbed, and when the police boarded the train, they wouldn't let her leave because they thought she had seen what had happened, but she had been asleep and didn't even know the man sitting next to her was dead. They sat on this train in the jungle for fifteen hours before the police allowed them to leave. She was one tough young woman, and that's an understatement.

Laura, the pink, spiked-haired girl, and I took a day and walked to Puerto Banus, not knowing how far it really was. This is where all the rich and famous from Europe come to show off their money. It was a beautiful spot but very, very expensive. The marina was filled with enormous cruise boats, and the place reeked of big money.

We stopped at an art gallery where Laura had an interview to nanny two children. The mother and the kids loved her, but the artist father, thought she was too showy to be taking care of his children. He told her, she had to do something about the stupid hair, and it didn't matter if the kids liked her or not, he didn't. He was a nasty egocentric man, and I was glad she decided not to work for him.

His gallery was totally bizarre. This man had paintings that cost over a million U.S. dollars, and then had his children's paintings hung right beside his own. He wanted thousands of dollars for his little kid's paintings! What the hell, they were no better or no worse than his. He wanted to know if I would like to work for him as a sales agent, but when I didn't have any legal papers that quickly ended. The truth of the matter was he thought I was German, and most of his clients were from Germany. He was super rude when I told him I was from the U.S. and didn't speak German. He turned his back on me and sort of huffed off, as if I were no longer worthy of his time. I wouldn't have lasted one hour working for that arrogant ass. Laura and I had a jolly good laugh, and then caught a taxi back to our hostel. We had both decided it was time to continue our journeys. Laura was off to Paris, and I was going farther south to see what was to be seen. But I sure will remember that pink-haired friend.

Having made the decision to travel south, I bought a ticket, and the next bus stop was Malaga. Oh my God, it was a dirty, nasty town! Even if there were a school that wanted to hire me, I didn't want to live there. Crazy as it may have been, I saw a huge cruise ship docked in the harbor, and I thought why not try and see if I could get a job on the ship? It was a strange idea, but I guess I just wanted out of Malaga so badly that I'd try anything.

I asked some people who worked on board about getting a job on the ship, and they contacted the main man for hiring. He took me aboard and showed me the entire ship, but then he told me that hiring was done in Austria, or I would have to wait until my legal papers cleared in Spain. This was crazy, because I had never dreamed that it would even be possible to get hired on this or any cruise ship in Europe. It was just one of those silly moments when you say to yourself, "What the hell, it might work, and if not it would be a good laugh." To this day I still giggle about the craziness of the moment approaching this huge ship with the idea of climbing aboard, and cruising off into the sunset. I almost did, but Austria seemed even to me, to be a long way from Spain to apply for some-sort of adventure. I thanked this kind man, and told him it was rather a bizarre idea, and laughingly left the ship.

It was time to make a decision. For the last week, I had been thinking about checking out Turkey. Travelers I had met along the way didn't think it was such a good idea. They all had negative things to say about Turkey, but especially wondered why a woman would want to go to a country where women were treated so inferior. I wondered what to do next; Turkey or not? I spent very little time deciding to leave Spain behind me. I thought of seeing more of Europe, but Mexico had spoiled me with its cheap prices, and now Europe just seemed outrageously expensive. Mainly, I missed the warm, friendly people of Mexico.

Looking out the airplane window, I said, "*adios*" to Spain. I was already feeling happier, and excited about my trip back to Seattle, and then on to somewhere in Mexico.

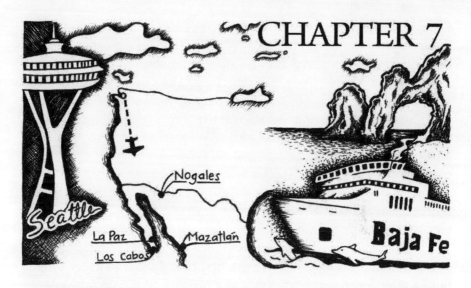

Once again I was returning to Mexico, but I wasn't sure where I would end up. I'd informed my daughters not to worry, that anywhere in Mexico was going to be more fun and much easier than Spain. I booked a ticket to Los Cabos and was excited to try my new teaching and traveling wings. Los Cabos was the easiest place to fly into on the Baja Peninsula, but I didn't intend to stay there. My plans were to spend a few days of vacationing and then go on to La Paz, which a world traveling friend had recommended.

Los Cabos was just a small strip of new hotels along the ocean, the main town being Cabo San Lucas, which was close by. I caught a taxi with a group of foreigners to Cabo San Lucas. However, upon arriving, after an hour of looking around I decided to keep going. I checked at the bus station for a quick trip out, and within an hour, I was on another bus for La Paz. This area just didn't feel right for me. All I saw were enormous, luxurious hotels and trendy restaurants; McDonald, Burger King, and Taco Bell. My God can you imagine Taco Bell in Mexico? Then at the edge of all the luxury were tin shacks and rubble, where the local people of Mexico lived. I just didn't like the idea, that this beautiful place had been taken over by big money, and that the Mexican families were pushed aside to live side-by-side with all that luxury in their face.

It was about a three-hour bus trip from Cabo to La Paz, and it was the coldest bus in the world with their air-con on full blast. I certainly wasn't prepared with all my clothes locked in the baggage compartment below. As I sat shivering, the best I could do was snuggle up to my big purse draped over my arms for a little added warmth, and try to move away from the freezing air. I was a happy woman to arrive in La Paz, and be greeted by the sun, and temperatures in the 90s.

La Paz is a city of 200,000, but it still felt like a small fishing village to me. I found a room at the Hostel Del Convento, not a great room, but the location was near the *Malecón* (the sea wall, usually the main area in a coastal town). It was also surrounded by small shops and restaurants, making everything easy to find.

While I was eating breakfast the first morning, a waitress wanted to exchange English classes for Spanish. Then all the waiters told me they needed English lessons also. Things already looked appealing, and everyone was friendly and happy, plus the food was so much better than in Spain.

After a wonderful, big breakfast, I walked the length of the *Malecón*. It was a lovely walkway with trees and plants facing the bay of La Paz. In the middle of the *Malecon*, was a long wooden dock at least a hundred feet in length, extending out over the water. There were perhaps a dozen young boys fishing, and I saw hundreds of little brilliantly colored fish. I could hardly wait to get in the water. But, I first needed to find a clean beach because the water off the *Malecón* was horribly polluted from cargo ships. La Paz was a huge shipping port, and to get to a decent beach you needed to travel about 30 minutes from the city center.

Later that week I spent an afternoon looking at different schools, and they did need teachers here but, not until August since right now was everyone's summer vacation. I definitely needed to learn that schools had schedules, instead of thinking I could just pop in any old time, and find a job that same week. The ESL schools weren't closed, but they only had a handful of students. Just for the fun of seeing what the various schools had to offer, I spent a day taking my resume to different ones.

I was hired at one of the schools by a remarkable young couple that taught at the University. They had just started an ESL school, and needed three or four teachers starting the middle of August. I had to be honest with them, and tell them I wanted to see what Mazatlan had to offer, but I'd let them know as soon as I knew what I wanted to do. I knew I would love to work for them, but August was a few months away, and it seems difficult just to hang around La Paz with no job. That evening they took me to an elegant restaurant for dinner, where I met their daughter and several of their friends. I was tempted to say yes; they were such intriguing, educated people, and had exciting new ideas for their school. But---.

My main problem with La Paz was that I truly wanted to be right on the beach, so I could enjoy it with ease every day and not have to take a 30-minute bus ride. It seemed a little weird to think I was that big of a beach bum, but it was the determining factor of where I'd hang my hat, even for a short time. After all the years of freezing in Montana, Alaska, and Washington, I craved the sun, the beach, and the lovely ocean.

The other school that I interviewed at was totally bizarre. I was required to take a personality test which took about an hour and had some pretty strange questions. One question asked, how do you feel about prayer in schools? Another was, who do you think is more important the Pope, Madonna, or Bon Jovi? What the hell sort of crazy question is that? I didn't say the Pope. I chose Bon Jovi. I always liked their music, and I wasn't sure which Madonna, they were asking about. Prayer in schools would be okay, as long as I didn't have to lead it. I finished the test just because I wanted to hear what they had to say. They looked the test over and quickly informed me that they didn't think I would work well with their school. I agreed. It wasn't for me, and I still laugh about that test. I didn't know that there were ESL schools like that! After that interview, I decided I'd definitely go to Mazatlan to see what it was like.

I'd met a couple of young backpackers, Nigel and Ellen from Ireland at my hostel, and we were taking the ferry to Mazatlan together. When we boarded the ferry, I noticed everyone else had blankets or sleeping bags. Those people knew things we didn't.

When it is 95 degrees outside, who would think they would ever be cold within a few hours? We were so chilled by midnight that we were up walking around just trying to stay halfway warm. I finally found a little spot down in the cafeteria next to some sort of heat coming from the engine, and away from the cold night air. After freezing all night, I wished I had splurged on a nice, warm cabin, but I didn't know it would get that cold in the tropics. As we pulled into the bay of Mazatlan, I was happy to see the sun come up. There were at least a dozen dolphins following the boat which I believed to be a sign of good fortune.

The three of us set off on foot to find a cheap hostel. We walked the whole damned town, or so it seemed, because the hostels were either too expensive or Ellen didn't want to stay there. Finally, Nigel and I told her, "We have had enough! We're taking the next halfway decent place, no matter the cost. We can all share a room and make it cheap for all of us." We lucked out and found a nice, clean, and inexpensive hotel. Ellen, in the meantime, had decided she didn't want to share a room and wanted to stay alone. Nigel and I were ready to ditch her as she had become a real pain in the butt. The two of us took a room together, and quickly left for the beach. He was leaving in the morning for Zihuatanejo and then on to Belize, so we needed a *buen viaje* (have a good trip) drink.

Ellen and I accidentally met up on the beach the next day and while eating breakfast she told me, "Donna, after traveling with you and seeing how you are living, I have a problem." Oh, good God; I was wondering why I was sitting there with that girl. I hadn't come this far to hear someone bitch me out.

Then she looked at me and quietly said, "The reason I stayed alone was to take some time to try to figure out what to do with my life. I think I'm pregnant." She told me her story of having an abortion when she was twenty, and swearing that if it ever happened again, she would be prepared to deal with it.

Looking like a lost child, she said, "But, now you make me want to keep going on my own journey. If I'm pregnant and have a child, may I name her Donna after you, a lady on a journey all by yourself?" With tears in her eyes she told me, "You love life so much that I want to see another Donna with a smile and on her own journey." Then we bought a pregnancy test and cried a few private tears together.

My two friends departed and I started looking for ESL schools. Whenever I wanted to find ESL schools, the first thing I always did was check the yellow pages. Then I'd normally go to a local bar where the bartender spoke English, and ask their opinion as to the best schools. Bartenders usually speak English, and they know what is happening in their town. At least I've had good luck with it. So with my list of schools in hand, I looked for a cute sidewalk bar.

I already had an interview at Institute English, so I asked the bartender what he thought. He warned me that the man who owned it had a bad reputation of not paying his teachers. The owner would tell you he would pay you every week, but then it would be next week, and next week, until you just quit. I went there anyway, and sat in on a class, but it was pretty awful as the teacher spoke seventy percent Spanish, and the students obviously weren't happy. I later had a friend who worked there, and was never paid, quitting after teaching a month for free. Sometimes you just get lucky, but more likely I should have thanked the bartender for the heads-up.

I took a job at Active English, which the local people thought was the best school. The lady who owned the school had an apartment for rent, and it was only $150 USD a month. I took it sight unseen as the other teachers told me it was quite nice. The director of the English department also lived in the same apartment building, so I thought that should be beneficial. I now had a job and an apartment after only three days in Mazatlan.

My new apartment was more than adequate, but a twenty-minute bus ride from school. It was truly at the edge of town, so it wasn't easy for me to get to the beach, and that was why I had wanted to live in Mazatlan. I knew I had to look for something closer to the school, and the beach very soon.

The first day in my apartment I met the handy-man who lived downstairs. Luckily, for me he spoke a little English, as my Spanish was still lacking. It was a good thing I met him because when I went to open my door to go outside, the door knob fell off. The knob was lying outside the door, so there was no way to open it. What to do? I looked out my window and saw a lady in the courtyard next to our building. I got out my dictionary and then yelled to her, "*Señora, por favor, vaya a* Charlie Brown*, mi puerto, no abierto, necesito ayudar* (Please, get Charlie Brown. My door won't open, and I need help)." I wasn't sure she understood my Spanish, or had gotten the message, but in a little while, Charlie Brown showed up with tools, and we started trying to get me out. He worked for about an hour but to little avail. I was just sitting on my side telling him what a terrific job he was doing, and how I appreciated his efforts. Finally, he got a screwdriver through the doorknob hole, and I removed the hinges, and he then knocked the door down. Thank God, I had remembered his name! Well, who wouldn't remember a Mexican with the name Charlie Brown?

A few days later, as I started to climb the stairs to my apartment, I switched on the light, and there was a huge tarantula. Well, to me it was huge—the size of a small saucer. I screamed and screamed! No, I'm not one of those women who scream, but this thing totally freaked me out. A man in the restaurant next door, who had heard my piercing screams came and killed it. He assured me it wasn't a poisonous one, in fact it was sort of nice and ate lots of nasty bugs. He told me, he knew what was wrong by the sound of my scream, because it sounded like his wife when she saw a tarantula. It was my first time seeing one, and I hoped it would be my last. No such luck, in fact, walking to my bus I usually saw at least one of those horrid critters. They had definitely made me want to move closer to town, where everyone said there were fewer of them.

I started teaching at Active English and only had three hours, but I thought it was okay, for the time being. The teachers there were all happy with their jobs, and appeared to be good teachers, and likeable people. After being there only one week, the English director a Canadian man, told me he was going to Korea to teach, but to not to tell anyone because his Mexican wife didn't know. He left his pregnant wife with her family and headed off to Korea. I guess not everyone at the school was that nice.

He was quickly replaced by a lovely Canadian woman. She and I become friends right away, and happily she gave me as many hours as I wanted. I was teaching five hours a day, and that was perfect. I had classes of beginners, and also advanced, so I could clearly see where it was possible to take these students in a few short months. I was already in love with my students, plus I had found a sweet little apartment close to the school.

I made friends with a group of guys at the corner bar, and I'd stop after class, and we'd play dominoes together. They didn't speak any English, but somehow with my Spanglish, we all understood each other, the game, and the little jokes. The bartender spoke great English, and this was how I got invited to play with them. He told the guys, I would help them with their English, and so they welcomed me. The English lessons were minimal, and all we did was laugh, drink beer, and poke fun at whoever lost the game. It is amazing how you can make friends without even speaking the same language, but it sure happens.

One day the bartender asked me, where I lived. When I told him, he said, "Be very careful in that neighborhood."

"No, no I live right there," and pointed to my street. "It's a very nice neighborhood, maybe one of the nicest."

"Yaw, it's nice because that's where all the rich drug dealers live. Do you sometimes hear a bang, bang, at night? Well, that noise is guns. The druggies are trying to kill each other, and they all live next to you."

Yes, there were shootings during the day and downtown, but I had never thought it could happen in my sweet little neighborhood. Now I looked at my neighbors with a little different view; I still couldn't believe it, because they were all so nice to me, and their families seemed very normal. I did know I wouldn't be going with them to Sunday dances in the country-side, in their expensive, new, fancy black vans with darkened windows, ever again. But, those Sunday dances had been so entertaining with everyone from the countryside attending. They had all loved dancing with the only *Gringa* there. Men and women had tried to teach me to dance like a Mexican, shaking my shoulders instead of my butt, and we had all laughed, drank toasts to each other, and laughed some more. I would miss those dances. I thanked the Universe that had looked out for me, it must have been working over-time on my Sunday dances in the countryside.

Monica, the owner of our school, was married to a *vaquero* (a cowboy). I told him, in my best Spanish that his saddles were beautiful. Truthfully, his saddles were amazing works of art. The base was made of hand carved wood, to fit a certain horse, then hand-tooled leather covering the wooden base. The leather was beautifully overlaid with elegant silver work on the side panels. I shouldn't have told him how elegant his saddles were because then he thought I loved horses also.

"No," I told him, "I was raised on a ranch, but I hate to ride horses." I guess he just couldn't believe that anyone raised near horses wouldn't love them. So now I had a date to go with him and his son for a Sunday ride. I thought it might be sort of fun, even though I didn't like riding, but I believed we were going to ride in the mountains. Instead of the mountains, we went to his stable, saddled up, and rode through the town with dogs barking and kids pulling on the horses' tails. It was at least 95 degrees, and may have been the worst horseback ride in history. You had to love a man, who loved to ride his horse even in brutal heat, and on the city streets, no less.

I was extremely impressed with his horsemanship and his horses. These majestic horses were the type of Mexican horses that you see in the movies or on TV, that dance. It was quite exciting for me because, with just the nudge of the knee it would switch its back legs, and with a tap of the toe, it's whole rear end would swing. I have to say it made even me look like a great horse-lady. He insisted that next Sunday, I needed to have a saddle for a lady. Oh, my God, I had seen them, and they were sidesaddles! This was more dangerous for me than the gangsters on my street ever thought of being. If friends in Montana could see me now, they would get a good laugh at the girl that loved fast cars, and not horses.

I did win the heart of his son that day with my talk of living on a ranch, and my brother who used to be in rodeos. Until then, Monica's son wouldn't take English lessons at his mother's school. Now he was my private student, and it made me feel like a master teacher. We had amusing classes about horses, cows, barbed wire or anything about ranches. I'm sure he spoke perfect English at the rodeos, but that was about all I could get him to talk about. Hey, even in a foreign country, if the boss is happy, just keep doing what you're doing!

One day at school all the teachers were talking about taking their *parasito* medicine. When I asked what it was, they all looked at me like I was a real dummy. They explained; after you had been in a third-world country for a few months you really needed to take medicine to get rid of the parasites and amoebas. Then they told me how they knew they needed to take a dose. One of them had a slight headache every morning, and one had an ache in her arm. Since I had been having a nagging, little headache daily, I thought it was a good idea to try it. It worked for me, and I had no more headaches. A friend in Mexico joked, "Don't people in the United States eat meat, vegetables from the ground, or sit on the sidewalk? What, is the U.S. so super clean they have no parasites?" Since then I have taken my medicine every six months, or as directed by the pharmacy.

On the morning of September 11th, I had an eight o'clock class with eight women students. One or two of them were always late, so when one of them came in late I wasn't surprised. Unlike her, she interrupted class, and told me in an extremely nervous voice, "Teacher, an airplane hit a big tower, in the United States!" I politely thanked her for telling us, and continued with my class. She kept looking at me as if I were doing something wrong, but I continued with class anyway.

When class was over, I went to the front office, and saw everyone hanging around the television. It was showing the first plane hitting the World Trade Center, just like she had told me, but all that time I had been thinking of a water tower. At least I had told her it was very sad, and I hoped no one had been hurt.

We all remained glued to the TV, and everyone was telling me they were so sorry for my country. I told the director, I was going up the street to a bar with television in English, and everyone went with me. We spent the day watching this horrid tragedy. Many people who I didn't even know told me how sorry they were for my country, and that they were glad I was safe in Mexico. Like everyone in the world, we waited anxiously for a few weeks to see if anything else would happen. Like all bad times, it passed, and life returned to normal. I'm not sure I ever regained the respect of the student, who had delivered the news that morning. I just hoped that she understood my confusion.

Almost every day my new friend Ernesto and I would go to the beach, the old part of town, the market, or just hang out at my apartment watching television. Ernesto, was from Zihuatanejo, and he was my friend Terry's, boyfriend. Terry was the new English director at our school, and she worked eight to ten hours daily. While she was working, Ernesto and I played. I only worked two hours in the morning and three in the late afternoon, and Ernesto worked part-time at nights as a bartender, so our days were free to do whatever, we wanted.

Ernesto became my unpaid guide to Mazatlan. He was an extremely intelligent man, who had learned his English talking to Terry in Canada on the telephone. With his fluency in English and Spanish, plus his wonderful personality, he was the best tour guide I could have ever had. We both liked to explore Mazatlan, and he showed me the highs and low of the city. Without Ernesto, I would have missed much of Mexico's real life. I was so lucky to know both of them, and they kept me dancing, drinking, and laughing until the wee hours many nights.

On one of those late nights Ernesto and I decided we should become blood-brothers. Neither of use had a knife, thank heavens, but we did find a rusty, dirty nail, and with some scratching we both had enough blood to proclaim, "W*e are now bonded in life by our blood.*" The next morning neither of us thought that had been such a brilliant idea. A week later we both had a nasty infection from the rusty nail, and today I have a small scar to prove it. But this boy is still my brother, at least in blood.

My crazy Mexican brother also taught me to whiff vodka. Some wild bartender on the beach had made this a big hit with the younger crowd, and so of course we had to try it. First, you make a little pocket between your thumb and pointer finger, pour a bit of vodka in, and plug one nostril, and sniff with the other. I will guarantee you the first thing anyone will say is "Oh, shit!" Why do you do this? I have no idea, maybe just to do it. It was crazy and a little painful, but just one of the fun times with Terry and Ernesto.

One day Ernesto and I were walking down the beach, and I told him, "Let's go through this hotel, and we can cut across to my house easier."

Ernesto wasn't hot for this idea, but I kept pushing him, and finally he told me, "They won't let me go through the hotel."

"What are you saying, Ernesto?"

"Donna, they won't let me go through the hotel. I'm a Mexican, and they won't let me in there."

I had never been so upset, and I insisted that we try. He was right; they stopped us at their gate. Glaring at them, I said, "Oh no it's okay, he's with me."

With a glare of their own, they replied, "No, he isn't allowed, and now neither are you."

Well, have you ever heard a Montana girl call someone every word her mama told her never to say? I used every one of those words and a few extra. To this day, it makes me so angry and so sad for the way he was treated in his own country. Those guards were Mexican, and the most I could hope for them was that they hated their jobs and had to work long, long hours for little pay, and developed huge warts on their faces.

One of the best laws in Mexico is that all beaches are public, and all Mexicans can use any beach. Our problem that day was a private business can stop anyone from entering their property. I did learn to listen to my Mexican friends, and when they said to do or not to do something, I followed their directions.

One morning I woke with a terrible pain in my back. It so happened that my landlady was going to see a chiropractor that morning, and she invited me to come along and see if he could help. I went with her, and he gave me an adjustment, but the next morning I was in much worse pain, and had a strange rash across my chest and back.

Returning to his office, it struck me, somehow I knew I had shingles. I asked him about it, and he thought that was probably correct, because his wife had experienced the same thing, and she had been diagnosed with shingles. For the next three weeks, I had stabbing pains in my chest, and across my back. It was a little difficult to teach when suddenly it felt like someone stabbed me in the chest with a knife, and tears would come to my eyes. My wonderful friend Terry would come over twice a day, and smear my back with some magical cream that the pharmacy had recommended.

A short time later I also had toenail fungus. My students told me what it was, and warned me it would take a long time for it to go away, unless I took a certain pill. They also explained the pill was rather dangerous, but nothing else worked as fast. Again, the pharmacy sold me a cream, and said it was very normal for that to happen in the tropics. This was such a lovely sight, as my nail turned black, and sort of deformed. This ugliness took about a year to get rid of, even using every remedy known to man.

Then the tattoo on my ankle developed warts, lots and lots of little warts. My poor old crab tattoo looked like it was molting. My friend suggested I stop at the pharmacy because a doctor came there daily, and I could talk to him. When I arrived, I told him my problem, and showed him my new warts. He looked my tattoo over and told me, " *Es necesario cortar* " with a slash of his hand. I understood, he needed to cut them off.

"Que? Las veragas?"(What? The warts*?)*

"No, no necesario cortar tattoo, usted tienes veneno en su sangre. Es posible muerta mañana, el veneno va a corazón, y boom! Muerta." This was all said with lots of hand motions, and I got it. I needed to have my tattoo removed, cut off, or the poison in my blood would kill me, maybe even tomorrow, boom dead. The lady that ran the pharmacy was listening, and her eyes were as big as saucers. She was almost as dubious as I was. I thanked them both, and told them, *"Hasta mañana* y gracias"(I'll see you tomorrow and thank you).

Then I walked up the street to another pharmacy and showed my tattoo to the pharmacist there. All he said was, "Warts, use this ointment, and they'll go away." Second opinions are always good, no matter what. I still have my tattoo, and wish I had more of that cream, whatever it was, because those ugly warts disappeared in a week or so. The pharmacist explained, that this hot and humid weather was not something my body was used to after living in cold climates. My body needed to make adjustments, and I might have more strange problems later on. Pharmacies are one of the great things in Mexico, just go to one where you like what they tell you.

When not hanging out with Ernesto, I spent my free time with another Mexican friend, Fela, who was known as the flower lady. She made crepe-paper flowers by the hundreds, and was teaching me to make them with her. It was great fun sitting with her making flowers, and practicing my Spanish. She was not only a delightful conversationalist, but a darn good con artist, as she always had a sad story to tell about no food, or no money for rent, or a sick child. You had to appreciate her efforts as she had compelling stories, and a different problem every day in case you had heard the old spiel. Hey, here I was making flowers for her to sell, so I guess she did a good con job on me, too.

I had been at Active English for five months when Monica, the school's owner, announced that all the foreign teachers had to get their FM3. This would cost $300USD, and we had to do it that week because the government was coming back to check. The FM3 (similar to a "green card" in the U.S.) is the legal work paper for foreigners in Mexico. Sad to say, but all the foreign teachers, myself included, told her we couldn't do that. We would have to work months to make up the $300USD, with a salary of six dollars an hour. None of us understood why she didn't just pay the *mordida* (bribe), as was the normal procedure in Mexico, but she wasn't. I went to class that night, and told my students good-by, and explained why I was leaving. When none of the other foreign teachers arrived for class, the school erupted into complete turmoil, the students were extremely upset that these teachers were all leaving. This left only the Mexican teachers (which were very good), but the reason our students attended was to have teachers whom English was their first language. Monica's office was full of outraged students. These students knew it was a normal process to pay the officials a bribe, and that would be the end of the school's problem. I quietly listened to a few of her excuses, then slowly made my way to the door, hugged some of the students, and waved good-bye. I met the other teachers in the parking-lot, who were all waiting to hear the gossip. We all had to decide what we were going to do next. I decided I'd go back to Zihuatanejo because it was familiar and fun. This wasn't a problem to me as I love changes.

My friend Terry did have a problem. She had a car, and it had to return across the Mexican border every six months, and that time was fast approaching. Still being in Mazatlan, it made sense for her to go to Nogales, Arizona the closest border city, which was a ten to twelve hour trip. She didn't want to travel alone, so she asked if I would go with her. I thought it would be entertaining, and I truly didn't want her to go alone. Ernesto had met Terry in Nogales when she drove from Canada the first time. He had spent three days waiting for her to arrive holed up in a motel on the Mexican side of Nogales. He ranted and raved about how horrid it was, and how afraid he was to leave the motel room. After I had listened to Ernesto talk about Nogales, I felt a little nervous, but obligated to go with her, because he sure wasn't going to go. So we made plans to leave the next morning.

The day didn't begin exceptionally well. Problem number one, when Terry tried to start her car the battery was dead. Then she had to wait for the bank to open. I have good instincts, and my vibes were telling me this was not a smart idea, but my heart overruled, and I climbed in next to Terry.

Once on the road, I knew my instincts had been right. I couldn't believe I had accepted this adventure, and was now riding with the fastest driver in all of Mexico. Our only stops were for gas, food, and occasional potty breaks. We also had the obligatory military checkpoints every hundred miles or so. There were several of these checkpoints along the way, and we had to pull in while young soldiers with machine-guns stood guard over us as we opened the trunk of the car. They were always very nice, and polite, but wanted to spend a little extra time looking, because Terry is an extraordinarily beautiful, young woman. Plus she has massive boobs, is an outrageous flirt, and speaks great Spanish. I was sure no other cars were delayed as long as ours, but I was happy for the stops as it gave me a few minutes peace from the wild ride.

Driving in the daytime was sort of scary with her, but driving at night in Mexico is a thrilling experience in itself, as this is when the cows, burros, and people all use the highway. So with Terry's record-breaking speeds, it is sort of like playing dodge ball. It is certainly not recommended by the AAA, or by me! Terry is from Saskatoon, Saskatchewan, Canada where the roads are straight, and there are many miles in between towns, so speed was a normal thing to her. I don't think they have burros, cows, and people on the roads at night there, though.

After about ten or eleven hours of traveling with my young speed demon, we were in Nogales at the official border between Mexico and the U.S. A large sign said, "Shut off engine, present passport, present visa." They didn't even look at me, or my passport, they just hit it with a stamp and said, "Welcome home, you are now entering the United States of America." As for Terry, they were all standing around, and smiling like a cat got their tongue, and waving for her to go ahead.

But—R_R_R_R_R_R, the car wouldn't start! R_R_R_R_ -- she kept trying, but it was getting less and less likely that it was ever going to start. The border guard told us to wait in our car. After fifteen minutes or so a guard from the U.S. and a guard from Mexico were still trying to decide which country we were in, Mexico or the U.S? We needed a tow-truck, but from what country? If we could decide we thought it would be cheaper in Mexico, but may take longer. What about getting parts if they are needed? Who had the best mechanic? Well, the border patrol finally made the decision. Your car must cross the border by tomorrow, each country agreed, and they pushed us into the U.S.

Strangely, a tow truck came from the Mexico side and towed us to a garage in the U.S, where her car sat for three days. We knew it wasn't the fastest service, but we hoped it was the best, as it is a long way between service stations on the Mexican highways. Several days later the car was ready and so were we. Nogales, Arizona in November was cold, rainy, dirty and not a pleasant place to be. We spent most of our time eating, playing cards and watching American TV, both anxious to get out of there. We clearly had stayed the required seventy-two hours before her car could return to Mexico.

Buen Viaje! Read the sign as we left the United States crossing into Mexico. Our personal papers were stamped in about five minutes, and Terry's car had a new sticker (which was what was needed), and we were off to Mexico again with my little Mario behind the wheel. I know it would have been easier for me to go to Mexican Immigration for an extension on my visa, but I would have missed an exciting experience, and I'm glad my friend wasn't alone. I also learned that I didn't want to own a car while I was living in Mexico, and I wasn't even sure I wanted to know anyone with a car.

Nine or ten hours later, we arrived back in Mazatlan, and I felt as if I should kiss the ground, and perhaps consider going to church on Sunday.

All the foreign teachers from Active English were going to Zihuatanejo. I didn't know what we all planned to do there for jobs, as there weren't that many schools. I just hoped that Donilo needed a teacher, but if not, perhaps it was finally time to go to Costa Rica or farther south. I wasn't worried about the others as they were young, creative and didn't need a baby-sitter.

I needed to pack and catch the bus to Zihuatanejo, which I had done before. But, this time I would just lay back and not worry about the young, crazy driver, as it would seem like a snail's pace after my trip to Nogales.

CHAPTER 8

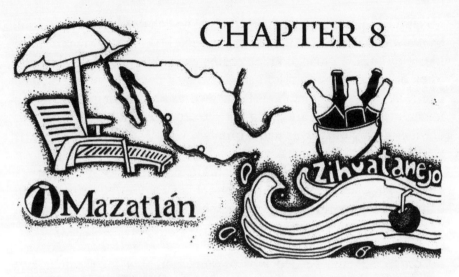

One year ago I started my journey in Puerto Vallarta, and now I was celebrating my 58th birthday as we passed through it on my way back to Zihuatanejo. It's a 24-hour trip from Mazatlan to Zihuatanejo, but I was genuinely excited to be returning.

Cory (another teacher from Mazatlan) and I were taking the bus to Zihua. I warned him that it was one hairy, long, and windy road. Most of my reminiscing was about the one stop we would make, and my story got longer the closer we got to our lunch break. As I was telling Cory the *"sopa de camarón"* story, my mouth was watering in anticipation of this delicious-looking soup. I warned Cory that when we got to the restaurant, he was on his own, because, this time I was getting my shrimp soup.

Soon the bus stopped at the little café that I coveted, and everyone was pushing off the bus, and hurrying into the restaurant. I was determined to be first in line, and I quickly jumped off the bus. However, in Mexico there is no such thing as a line, it is who ever is the most aggressive. You guessed it, when I finally placed my order, "Sorry no more *sopa de camarón*, sorry no more tamales." Oh, hell, just give me a beer. Cory was lucky and got a ham and cheese sandwich. I was now sure that *gringos* didn't get to have the *sopa de camarón*, even if there was some left over. It would be six more hours to Zihua, so I quietly sat, and sulked over no shrimp soup.

Happily back in Zihuatanejo, I suggested that we go to the Hotel Cartier. I remembered it was a pleasant little hostel owned by a likeable Canadian man, and the rooms were always clean and cheap. They only had one room left, so Cory and I decided we could share one room. I'm not sure how I had evolved to sharing rooms with young men, but when traveling with backpackers, it had just worked out that way. They never had a problem with it, and neither did I. It was just the way it was.

My old friends at the Arcadia had lots of questions about Cory. I knew what they were thinking, and I had a lot fun letting them believe he was a boyfriend, with emphasis on the boy. Those Latino men always think every woman has to have a man by her side, or she couldn't possibly be happy.

Cory and I both needed jobs of some sort, but for the first few days we just hung out at the beach and played cribbage with Duane, the owner of Hotel Cartier. I also visited with all my old friends. Then I got serious and went to see Donilo, my friend who owned one of the ESL schools in Zihau. He didn't have anything for me right then, but he was sure someone would be leaving soon, and then the job would be mine.

My old friend Davy and I spent the day looking for an apartment. If I was going to stay in Zihua, I needed my own apartment, and Davy was the man to find it for me. He was the man you went to for any help you needed. He found me my first teaching job here and had also helped me with my Spanish. We found a cute place with the best patio in town, and a magnificent, new king-sized bed. My patio fronted the street, but with all the plants it was a secret, secluded, little garden, and yet I could still view all the street action. I loved it, and it was only $200USD a month, a good deal for such a perfect location, and the quality of the room. The price was thanks to Davy, because he talked the owner down from $300USD a month.

Davy also found Cory a cheap, nasty, fleabag flop for $50USD a month. Cory told me, "You shouldn't come to my house, unless you want to bring home bed bugs and lice, but I'm happy with my bed – bugs and the price."

Terry and Ernesto were sadly living with Ernesto's mother. Terry was having a difficult time living there, because there were RATS, lots and lots of RATS. She told me, "At night they make so much noise on the tin roof that I can't sleep, and when I go into the bathroom, there are herds of them, and they attack me." I thought this was pretty funny, until I went to visit them. It was even worse than I imagined, plus there were five adults and two babies living in one big room, with only a couple of curtains separating the sleeping areas. It was a pretty dismal situation.

I felt a little guilty about having a king sized bed with only one person sleeping in it and no rats. What could I do but invite them to stay with me? I went looking for Davy, and told him we needed another apartment, and quickly. Within a couple of days, Davy had found them an adequate apartment. Now that we all had somewhere to live, I needed to look for some kind of job until I could find one teaching.

One day I had no job and the next day I had two. They were both new to me, as I had never worked as a cook on a sail-boat, nor as a hostess in a restaurant/bar. In my very long life, I have been a hair-stylist, a travel agent, a house painter/sheet rocker, a farmer/rancher, an owner of a couple of art galleries, a housekeeper/cook/caretaker, a boat painter, and even a boat/house-sitter, but I had never worked in a bar/restaurant. The cooking job on a sail-boat sounded intriguing, but I decided on the hostess job instead.

When I lived here before, J.J.'s restaurant was the hottest spot in town. So I thought it would be fun to work as the hostess, with lots of potential for tips. Unfortunately, J.J.'s had a new owner and was no longer a sports bar, but now an expensive restaurant. Plus I quickly figured out that all the *gringos* in town were mad at the new owner for taking away their sports bar, so it wasn't the hottest spot in town any longer. However, I still took the job.

The owner was an extraordinarily wealthy, and ditzy German man from Mexico City, and he left me in command the first day. Well, like I said, I had never even worked in a bar or restaurant before, so how smart was this. I was the only *gringo*, and the other staff were local people. Everyone who worked there was exceptionally congenial to me except for the chef, who totally disliked me. I was supposed to critique his food, and change his menu. I didn't blame him for being angry with the new kid that didn't know squat, who was supposed to tell him, a chef, what was praiseworthy, and what he had to change. The best part was that I got to taste all the food, and if I didn't think something was particularly tasty, I told him the owner wanted it changed. I assured him I thought his food was fantastic, and some of it was. He made the best shrimp appetizers I had ever eaten: they were lightly sautéed prawns, placed upon a small dollop of garlic mashed potatoes, and topped with a drizzle of lobster bisque. This was my favorite, and I sold so many of these that finally the chef decided I was okay. It was no great love affair, but at least he didn't want to fry me for dinner.

One night a large group of people were enjoying dinner at J.J.'s. I heard a loud crash and looked into the restroom to see one of their friends was having an attack of some sort. I got the attention of the group, and the man was rushed to the hospital. Later I went to check on this group again and heard one of the women mention she was from Montana. I politely asked her, "Where in Montana are you from?"

She sort of shined-on my question with a curt reply, "Oh, you wouldn't know it. It's so small, people who live in Montana don't even know where it is."

I told her, "Try me, I know Montana pretty well."

With a slightly discussed look, she said, "I'm from a little town called Two Dot."

Smiling at her I replied, "Really, what is your last name?"

With a rolling of her eyes, she replied, "Baxter."

Being the smart-ass that I am, I said, "Oh and how are John and Mary Kay?"

I finally got her attention with that question, as those were the names of her parents. I told her that I had lived down the country road from her home, and knew all her family very well. I had been gone from Two Dot for years, so she being younger wouldn't know me, but she did know the rest of my family. She quickly got over her thoughts of my lack of knowledge for the area, and we had a fun evening talking over the latest gossip from Two Dot.

About a week later almost the same thing happened again with a young boy from Alaska, when I asked about his life and why he and a friend were in Mexico. He told me he was originally from

Montana, and pretty much the same exchange took place. I told him that I did know where he was from and that Martindale, where he had lived, was right down the road from Two Dot, where I was raised. We talked about people we both knew, and then I asked him what he was doing in Alaska? He was working on a fish-tender boat in Dutch Harbor. Having lived in Alaska for several years, I happened to know some of the men that fish in Dutch Harbor, and asked him if he happened to know Mike Clemens.

At that point, his eyes bugged out, and with a puzzled look, he asked me, "Just who the hell are you, and how do you know all these people?"

I explained that it was just a fluke, but that at my age I knew a lot of people. That seemed to satisfy him. However, I still wondered if maybe Zihuatanejo didn't have some odd, universal pull. It was extremely strange for two people from Two Dot, Montana to be in Zihua, and for it to come up in a conversation, and then for me to be there when they were talking about Montana. Two Dot is so small it isn't even on many maps.

Working nights at J.J.'s left my days free for the beach and friends, but it also meant late-night hours. My normal work schedule was 5PM-1AM. After we had closed, I would go down the alley to the Jungle where all my friends hung out or worked, and then sometimes, much later, I'd continue home.

One night during the Christmas holiday, when I arrived home, there was a young couple sleeping on my patio. I woke them because they had backpacks lain beside them, and I was worried they would sleep through being robbed. They told me, in Italian and a little Spanish, that they couldn't find a room, anywhere at any price, which I knew to be true for this time of the season. So when they saw my hidden patio, they sat down and hoped no one would care if they slept there.

I invited them to share my home, and my bed for the night. They were shocked, and I knew they were a little nervous. I assured them I wouldn't rob, rape, or murder them. We had a bit of a hard time communicating, as the Italian boy didn't seem to understand that I didn't speak Italian, but his girlfriend helped out with her little bit of Spanish.

We all spent the night in my splendid king-sized bed. I told them I would leave early in the morning, and please lock my door if they left before me. They were waiting when I got home, and treated me to breakfast, and then I took them to my friend's hostel, and begged him for a room. He didn't have a room, but he let them sleep on the couch in the lounge for a couple of nights. The next day they brought me a case of beer, and a lovely pair of turquoise earrings. They sure knew what would make me happy after only one night together. They told me I would always have a home in Italy, and if they weren't there when I telephoned, their entire family would know about Donna from Mexico, who shared her bed with them.

One of the best lessons I have learned on my journeys: if you have something someone needs, share it, and everyone's life will be better. I had a big bed, and that lovely couple had none. I wasn't crazy, and I didn't invite just anyone into my home or my life.. besides, if they robbed me the only thing there was to take were my clothes, some books, a couple of towels, and a few old dishes. Hey, it was Christmas, a time to give.

Lesson 45--- Share!

My patio had another guest who used it about twice a month. The first time I saw him, I was a little surprised and saddened. He was a boy of perhaps ten or eleven and exceptionally well dressed with expensive clothes and shoes, so I knew something was a little off for him. I got used to his sleeping in the corner of my patio every now and then, and when I came home, I'd quietly cover him with a blanket, and leave him a sandwich to eat. My only concern was that the lady I rented from might call the police, so I explained to her that he was my student, who had big problems with his father. I honestly believed that was why he slept there occasionally. I grew to miss him if he didn't show up when I thought he might. Strange enough, I never knew his name, and he just called me Teacher.

One day a creepy, dirty-mouthed man was standing in the street in front of my patio, screaming lots of vulgar words. Out of nowhere, my little friend and several of his buddies showed up. They ran him off, and I never saw the crazy man again. My little friend told me, that the man was *un hombre muy malo y loco* (a very bad, and crazy man) and that I should lock my door and stay away from him, but to call the police if he came back. I didn't know where those kids came from, but it sure was a sweet thing they did to protect me. Oh, how I hope that little boy has found a safe haven. He melted my heart in such a powerful way.

After being back in Zihua for a month, Donilo again yelled at me on the street, and asked, "Can you start teaching tomorrow?"

"Yes," I yelled back and giggled on down the street. I guess I was getting used to that way of getting a job from him. I was excited to have a job teaching again, but I still kept my hostess job at J.J.'s. I had classes from 8-10AM and again from 4-6PM. I worked it out with J.J.'s to run home, change clothes and get to work as soon as I could. Why was I working those senseless hours? Because it was so new and strange, and I didn't want to leave my friends at the restaurant. But I would never choose this over teaching.

One night after working late at the restaurant, I decided I would go home a little different way. As I was cutting through the back alley, a man yelled, "Teacher, what are you doing? You never come this way! We always watch for you because it is late, and we want you to be safe. I will tell my brother to watch for you, if you want to walk this way at night." I was teaching this man's nephew, and so he was my protector. Everyone in my neighborhood was related, so I knew the entire family. Where in this world does the neighborhood protect their teachers, except in Mexico?

It was December 31, 2001, and again I was ending a year in Zihuatanejo, but this year I was working, instead of playing. The night started off a little crazy, with a strange man fighting an imaginary bull with his imaginary cape, twisting, and turning, and yelling, *"Toro!" "Toro!"* This lasted at least half an hour, and we all knew that this poor man could truly see his bull. Sad to say, but our matador was hilarious entertainment, and certainly put us all in a festive mood.

When I finished at J.J.'s for the night, I stopped off at the Jungle, to wish everyone a Happy New Year. Then Ernesto, the waiters from Casa Bahia Restaurant and I went to Ixtapa, to complete our night with dancing until dawn. Coming home about 5AM, I was surprised by my landlady and her brother. They had drunkenly come to serenade me. My friend Terry (who had to work all night at the Jungle) also joined us for wine, tequila, and a jerked pork breakfast. You have to love those crazy Mexicans, and those crazy *gringos*!

Terry, Ernesto and I spent the next day recovering from slight hangovers, and then we decided to go get *pozole. Pozole* is a special-occasion soup in Mexico, especially in the state of Guerrero. It is a well-know cure for hangovers and is often eaten in the wee hours of the morning as a preventive, but it is also the traditional soup for the New Year. The soup base is usually pork or chicken with hominy in a red, green, or white broth, and comes with several small side dishes of cabbage, onion, avocado, oregano, radish, and of course chili, to add in the soup if you chose to.

We looked everywhere, and every restaurant was either full, or were out of *pozole*. As we were walking out of Pozole Alley, (a cute little alleyway of five or six restaurants that served traditional Mexican food) a *gringa* on a motor scooter hit the curb, and crashed right in front of us.

She was a mess, with terrible asphalt burns, and gravel embedded in her legs and arms, and blood all over her. But, her biggest concern was that the motor scooter was ruined. We took her, and the scooter back to my place to try to clean her up.

As I helped her into the shower, she wanted to know if I had an extra toothbrush. I thought maybe she had a brain injury if all she wanted to do was brush her teeth, but I gave her one anyway. Then she wanted to know if I would use it to get the gravel out of her skin. I did it, but it wasn't easy for me. I just closed my eyes, and started scrubbing. I couldn't believe what a mess she was, and here I was scrubbing gravel out of her cuts with a toothbrush. After getting her sort of cleaned up, off she went to party the night away. That is what we call, one tough woman!

A few days after meeting Kree, the crazy scooter girl; she, Ernesto, Terry and I opened Ernesto's mother's restaurant. Ernesto's mother had cancer, and there were days when she was just too sick to open her restaurant, or was in the hospital. We all decided to do this to help her out financially.

None of us knew anything about her restaurant, or what to prepare, but Ernesto thought we should cook some chicken, beef, rice, beans, and a salad. We all chipped in what money we had, and sent Ernesto off to the market to buy the meat he thought we should cook. Now we had to decide on the menu of the day, and who was going to cook what. I was designated the meat chef. Terry was the rice and beans girl. Kree would do the crispy fried plátanos that she had learned in a cooking school. Ernesto was our man to do what we told him to do, and get what we needed. Plus he needed to warn the locals that his mama's restaurant was open, and was being run today by some *gringo* girls, who only wanted to help his mama while she was in the hospital. We were all a little concerned that the local people would think a bunch of foreigners had taken her restaurant away from her while she was sick.

Most of our food turned out pretty decent, and the usual crowd that ate there seemed to agree that it was okay, but—not like mama's cooking. The nicest part was that all her customers left generous donations for her treatment.

After we cleaned the mess we had made of her restaurant. We delivered the news to her in the hospital, and gave her the donations. Tears were free-flowing from all of us. When she asked if she could hire us, we all laughed because we'd had a few mishaps that no one wanted to admit to, or repeat. We were a success that day, only because of all the kind people in her neighborhood that loved her, not because of our cooking. I heard one man say the meat was more like eating rubber than chicken, and that the rice was so sticky he could make it into a baseball—but he said it all with a huge smile.

My teaching job had taken priority over the bar/restaurant job, as I decided I was just too old to be doing all that late night, early morning rushing around. Besides having more hours at school, this was what I wanted to become "Great" at. I love teaching, and my students were the most prestigious job I could ever have. When I finish a day at school I feel like I had made someone's life better for his or her future, and that this is the best I have to offer this world.

My next-door neighbor was a young man named Asa. The reason I knew this was that every night a beautiful Mexican girl came and yelled, Asa, Asa! His room was way at the back of a locked hallway, and my apartment was in the front where she stood yelling, night after night. Getting sick of being woken up every night, I finally met young Asa from England. I informed him that he had to give that girl a key, or tell her to shut the hell up. I was familiar that in Mexico it was normal to stand and yell for a person when you want them to answer their door, but not at 3 o'clock in the morning. He thought I was pretty funny, and with that introduction, and a little time we became great friends. Every morning we shared my patio, Asa drinking his tea, while I had my coffee, sharing our Spanish dictionary or talking with Davy, our favorite Spanish teacher/friend.

Davy told us stories of his hellish childhood, but it sure hadn't affected his kind heart. Davy grew up in a pueblo south of Zihua in a family of twelve children. He had eight sisters and three brothers, but he was the oldest son. When he was only three or four years old, his father put him to work on the streets. He was taught to beg for money from the tourists, or steal whatever he could. If he didn't return home with at least thirty pesos, his father would remove his belt and whip him until he couldn't stand. Sometimes this was helpful because, for the next few days, he could show the tourists what would happen if he didn't bring home enough money. All the fathers in the village whipped their sons, but not like his father. His father seemed to enjoy it, and would check the bruises the next day, to see if he had whipped him enough. Davy thought his mother and older sister were lovely women, but he thought his father was the devil, or at least cursed by God.

Davy left home at age twelve. He didn't leave because of the whippings, he was used to those. He left to go north, to cross "the river"(the Rio Grande). On the streets, the older boys and men always talked of someday crossing "the river" and getting rich in *El Norte* (the U.S.). So at twelve years of age he started walking north. Some days he would get a ride for a short way with locals going to some pueblo in the countryside. Most of the people in these small villages were as poor as Davy, but they would usually share a small amount of food with him and at times a place to sleep. The best he could hope for was to get to a big city where there were tourists. That was where he could make money, and do what he had been trained; beg and steal from the tourists.

When he finally reached Guadalajara, he was tired, hungry, and depressed. He wondered if he'd ever make it to the river. He spent almost a year there living off the tourists and friends. Again, the talk on the street of *El Norte*, urged him on towards his goal. Davy crossed the Rio Grande when he was sixteen and once more when he was twenty-eight. Laughing, he said, "Some men could piss more water than what runs through parts of the mighty Rio Grande. Yet some of my friends are still there, never to try again." For a few, the goal was just to cross the Rio Grande, and prove that they were *un mucho hombre* and to have survived, but for most, it was the money. He laughed and said, "The *gringos* think we come to the U.S. for a better life. Ahh, what could be better than our sunshine, our tequila, and our beautiful women? Viva Mexico!"

On his first crossing, there was a group of men waiting for everything to be righ; the moon to darken, the patrols to pass, and then to make a run for it. Davy was in the water, and a good strong swimmer, but then one of the younger boys gave a whistle for help. No one stopped to help the boy, so Davy swam back to him. The boy was maybe nine or ten years old and couldn't swim. He was crossing all alone, so Davy did what lifeguards do, he grabbed him under his chin, and told him to pretend he was sleeping in his bed, and not to fight him. They made it across, and this little boy became like Davy's brother/son for the next three years. One of the first things Davy taught him was to swim. Even to Davy it seemed crazy to try to cross "the River" if you couldn't swim, but many men tried, and died there.

One day after talking about his crossings, he asked me, "Do you still like me, or like most *gringos*, do you think of me as a just a wet-back, trying to steal money from your country?"

"Oh! Davy, I think you might have been crazy, you could have died or been killed. You were so young and so very brave. You were only a little kid, and you walked 1,500 miles from your home, all alone! You are *un macho hombre,* to me."

He then asked, if I ever wrote in my journal about him. I told him, "Yes, but I don't ever tell anyone what we talk about."

I described what I had written about him. Then he sat up very straight and told me, "If you write this about me I would be proud to be included in your book, but I would never want my mother to know all the things I have done."

"Me neither, Davy. Who would?" We laughed, and I went to fix him a cup of coffee.

I heard a woman at the corner bar one day say, "Davy is Zihuatanejo! He's the first person I see when I arrive, and then not again until the day before I leave when he'll appear with his smiling face. Zihua just wouldn't be the same without Davy." My sentiments exactly.

One very late night, after hours of dancing with friends, Asa and I decided to go to Madera Beach for a swim. We grabbed a bottle of tequila, had a good swim and a few drinks. Pulled up on the beach was a sailboat where we decide to sit, and enjoy the moment while finishing our last drink, before walking back home. However, instead of going home, we took a *siesta*, a very long *siesta*.

At around 10AM my friend Marta, who owned the restaurant on Madera Beach, where the boat was anchored, woke me. As I slowly opened my blood-shot eyes, I looked out at tables full of people that I knew. They were all laughing and yelling "Bravo Donna, Bravo!" Marta's father was standing on the porch clapping his hands, and laughing. At that moment, I just wanted to curl up and die of embarrassment. This was my beach; I went there every day, I knew all the usual crowd of foreigners, the waiters, and Marta and her father were like my second family. Everyone there knew I was a teacher. What would they think now? Is she a drunk, and a baby snatcher by night, and a teacher during the day? I hoped they would all forget what they had witnessed.

Asa was young enough to be my son or perhaps even my grandson. If that wasn't bad enough, now we had to take the walk of shame past the Arcadia, where all my waiter friends would get to enjoy this little scandal also. It was fun having them wonder about my young friend Cory, but now Asa too. I'd never live it down. Asa thought it was all splendid fun. Had he no shame, spending a night on the beach with his grandmother instead of his beautiful young Mexican girlfriend? He laughed for weeks about our night on the boat, or I guess it was our morning on the boat. He thought the local beach gossip, that he was my new boyfriend, was a wonderful story, and more entertaining than if they were talking about his Mexican girlfriend. I just thought we'd better stick to coffee and tea from now on.

March was a terrible month for some of us in Zihua. My dear friend Duane, the owner of Hotel Cartier, lost his beautiful young wife. One day she was fine, and the next day she was seriously ill, and couldn't breathe. Duane immediately took her to the doctor, but she passed away in the office.

This was my first Mexican Catholic funeral, and it was so terribly sad and yet so beautiful. All funerals are sad, but when the horse-drawn carriage arrived with her casket, and the family walking behind, I was not the only one bawling like a baby.

In Mexico, when someone in your family dies, they are kept in the home, or in the funeral parlor. On the first night, the family, friends, and neighbors sit with the body and console the each other. On the second day or third day, the traditional funeral is held. Then there are nine days of mourning, with curtains closed, mirrors covered with black cloth, and the family stays home to comfort each other, without disturbances from others. After nine days, it is the end of the mourning period, and at this time, the family is supposed to continue with their life. Eight days before the one-year anniversary of the death there is another period of mourning, until the day of the anniversary. Then a mass is said to honor that person, and the family gathers to hold a fiesta and celebrate their life.

I celebrate your life Betty, and I hope this honors your memory. Zihuatanejo will always miss you.

Also, that month, I had a visit from a young and lovely sixteen-year-old friend, and her Grandmother. I was a little nervous when I saw them standing at my door, I could tell something was dreadfully wrong. They were both crying, and when I tried to console them my young friend told me, "I am so ashamed, but I need your help, I am with baby, and I don't know what to do." After hugging and trying to console her, I asked her if an abortion were possible in Mexico, and I thought Grandma might kill me right then. No, that was not an option.

It was a terrible situation, and more so because Cory, the teacher, and my ex-friend was at fault. I felt somewhat responsible because I had traveled with him, loaned him money, and had shared my home with this horrid person. When he found out she was pregnant, he quickly disappeared.

In Mexico, it is not an acceptable thing to be pregnant, and unmarried; it made the people see her as the town prostitute. If he would come back, and just live with her until the baby was born, it would make everything proper. This girl was the sweetest, and the most beautiful girl in Zihau, and well respected. So this time was extremely difficult for her family and friends. They pleaded with me to find Cory and convince him to come back. He didn't have to marry her. They only wanted him to stay until the baby was born, and then he could leave. It was simple, if he was there when the baby was born, no one would think poorly of her. They didn't want him to pay child support, or money for anything.

I looked everywhere for Cory, and all our friends were out searching. We all felt the same way, if we found him, he was going to see this girl and her family, and do what needed to be done. Or perhaps we'd have a big Mexican convince him to do the right thing, for this lovely girl.

This wasn't the first teacher I had known in Mexico that ran off and left a woman with a child. Warning to mothers—keep your daughters away from male ESL teachers, and educate them about sex! Or at least give them condoms.

This young girl and I became very close during this ordeal, and to this day we remain so. Some of my dearest friends I've met while traveling or stopping for a time somewhere. Sometimes the closeness ends then, and sometimes it lingers for years. It is simply a special bond formed by togetherness in abnormal situations and one of those rare gifts we sometimes receive.

Lesson 88--- Treasure your life and your friends.

It seemed that I was once again getting itchy feet. I wasn't sure if it was time to move on, or perhaps I needed to take my *parasito* medicine. I knew it was summer in Seattle, so I wouldn't freeze, and I felt it was time to visit my daughters.

CHAPTER 9

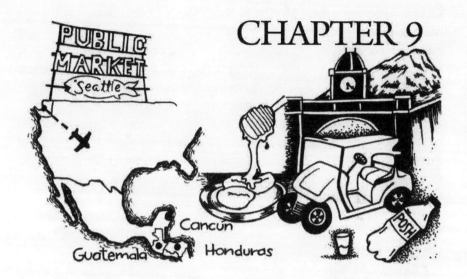

What do you mean we've been upgraded to first class? Oh my God, I don't know how my daughter did it, but first-class was superb: pillows, blankets, wine, and food, in fact, very good food. It was a long night flight from Seattle to Cancun, but this was heaven. Brandi and I had booked a short vacation together to Cancun, and another adventure onward to Guatemala for me.

Arriving in Cancun at 10AM, it was already shockingly hot, and difficult to breath. We hurried to our hostel and then set off for the beach. Like all photos of Cancun, it is one long strip of towering hotels for miles. It's easy to get to the beach, as you just go through any of those hotel lobby's, and out the other side, onto the beach. Yes, the sand is as white and water as blue as portrayed in the advertisements. It was spectacular, but the beaches were packed with people, and we preferred little remote beaches to these hordes of tourists.

We had read about a small island thirty minutes from Cancun. If the advertisements were half true, it sounded exactly like what we were looking for. We escaped Cancun and went in search of the ferry to this promised paradise.

Isla Mujeres was such a small island, we could drive a golf cart or scooter across it in twenty minutes. The water was as blue, and the sand as white as in Cancun, and the lack of people was much more desirable. Our hotel was new and ever so cute with only a few guests. Every day we rented our little golf cart from the people in front of our hotel, and took off for any beach we wanted. We would stop at the local store along the way, fill our cooler with cold beer, and then drive to the beach to watch the incredible iguanas.

There was a special spot at the end of the island, where an elderly man took care of iguanas. He fed them daily, and kept people away that would kill and eat them, as iguana is a traditional Mexican food, though now illegal. He was such a delightful old gentleman, and it was our favorite place to stop. Every day we visited him and his iguanas, and made a donation for their food and care. Then we would jump back into our little golf cart, and head to the next beach where we would stopped for lingua tacos, and a swim.

After all our fun days and nights, it was time for Bran to leave. I planned to stay and spend more time there though, because it was such a sweet little spot. She caught the ferry back to Cancun, and then a flight to Seattle, while I spent the next couple of days walking, touring the island in my speedy golf cart, and hanging out on the beach.

On September 19th, Hurricane Isadora hit Isla Mujeres and hit it hard. That was my first hurricane, and I thought it was pretty exciting. My hotel was on high ground, so there wasn't much to worry about plus it was a small, new hotel, and I felt completely safe there. It rained and rained and rained, and the wind got worse and worse. I was stuck in the hotel, as it was too dangerous to go out on the streets, because of electric wires breaking loose. The owner of my hotel checked on me daily, and told me that Isadore was gaining strength, so there wouldn't be any ferries for the next two days. I was thankful I had several good books, as there was no television, and at times no electricity. My room was beginning to feel smaller by the day.

On the 24th we were being hit by another hurricane, with water flowing through-out most streets. There was no electricity, and no ferries crossing to or from Cancun. The hotel owner told me I should catch the first ferry out, because the island was getting short of gas, bread, and no eggs anywhere. The ferry was supposed to dock the following day with some luck. It could cross the rough water; it just wasn't able to dock because of low tides during the day, and it couldn't hook to the landing.

The news on the island was; there were no flights out of Cancun, and all roads out of the city had also been closed. I decided to stay on the island until they were all out of beer and cigarettes. Why leave if I would be stuck in Cancun? I knew people had to get off the island for work, or other reasons, and I didn't have any reason for leaving. I had been warned another hurricane was expected. I decided hurricanes weren't my favorite thing, and they certainly had lost their intrigue. I braved the wind, and rain a couple of times a day just to stop from going stir crazy, but it certainly wasn't a smart move on my part. After seeing lightening strike and blow apart an electric transformer, I took cover and only went out for food and drink.

On the 30th the owner of the hotel was pounding on my door before daylight, telling me to pack my bags, and get to the ferry, now! I grabbed my backpack and raced to the dock. I was one of the first people there, so I felt positive about getting off the island. By the time the ferry arrived, I was way back in this pushing, shoving line. There had been fistfights, yelling, and lots of cussing, plus one man was shoved into the water. When the ferry docked it was a crazy mess, but I was on it.

Lesson 149---Hurricane parties blow

When we docked in Cancun, a man from the island told me to hurry to the hotel because he'd heard there was a severe shortage of rooms. I knew where the hostel was, so I took off running, as best I could with a huge backpack. Two separate *gringos* tried to stop me, wanting to borrow money. I guess things in Cancun had been more expensive, or their stay longer than their money held out. They both told me, "I'll bring you money, as soon as I get mine wired from the States." I had never seen *gringos* begging in Mexico before.

When I got to the hostel, there was only one bed left, and it was mine. The airport had opened, and a couple of roads leading out of town were open also, so things were beginning to improve, but this part of Mexico was a mess. The hurricanes seemed to have all blown over, and hopefully it would start to dry up. I laid back and enjoyed all the people stuck at our hostel, and as usual it was a colorful group with great stories to be heard.

My original plan was to go to the ruins of Tikal on the Mexican/Guatemala border, but the road was closed from the Mexico side. The report was that it would be a month or more before it opened because of landslides, and bridges that had been washed away. So I decided to take a bus to Palenque instead. The bus schedule said it was a 13-hour trip. I bought some snacks, a drink, and a couple of sandwiches and boarded the bus.

This trip from one coast of Mexico to almost the other coast wound through the jungle all the way. After sleeping, not sleeping, and then wondering why we were stopped, I needed to see what was happening. No one else seemed to care that we weren't moving. The old Mexican man sitting next to me told me, "No, no, don't go outside, it is too dangerous in the jungle."

When I asked him why we were stopped for so long he said, "We don't know, but soon someone will tell us." Well, I wanted to see what was happening, now.

To my horror, I saw hundreds of trucks, buses, and cars lined up on both sides of the road. I found out that a bridge had washed out, and we were waiting for equipment to come from somewhere. I don't know where the tractors came from, or how they repaired the road, but I do know we sat in the hot, muggy jungle for six hours, without moving. I think it took us about twenty hours total, but finally we arrived in Palenque.

I spent a little time checking out the few hotels that are in Palenque, which isn't a first-class city by any means, and decided Hotel Santo Domingo was the best, with clean sheets, and hot water. It was still a rather spooky hotel, but for $5USD who can complain. After I had been in my room for about five minutes, there was a knock on the door, and the night clerk wanted to know if I had an extra cigarette, or if I wanted to come have a beer with him. No *gracias*! Then I put a chair against the door for protection. I always have cigarettes, just not extra ones, and a drink with him was out of the question. I did sleep better knowing my trusty chair would at least make noise if someone tried to enter. This is the only hotel in my years of traveling that I ever did such a thing.

I arrived at the ruins at 8AM just when they were opening, and there were no other tourists yet. I was alone in the jungle, and it was total silence except for the monkeys hollering, and the parrots squawking. It was pure magic! I spent the entire day wandering the trails of the magical ruins, and felt the same wonder and sadness that I'd felt at other pyramids.

Traveling from Palenque for San Cristobal took about five or six hours. These buses are often held-up by banditos, and travel was advised for daytime only. I had no problems, but I'm a little disappointed not to have a story of banditos boarding my bus.

My only exciting bus story is; one night while on a long trip, somewhere, the bus stopped, and I jumped off to have a cigarette. As I jumped off the steps, two machine guns were shoved in my face. I didn't know if they were the good guys, or the bad guys, but they had guns, big guns, in my face!!! I had my cigarettes in my hand, and just started waving them around saying, *"Fumar, fumar, por favor"* They laughed, and wanted to know if they could have one of my cigarettes, and if I had a spare lighter.

San Cristobal was a charming little spot to take a break before entering Guatemala. It had lovely parks, great markets, and the county side was beautiful. The area is known for new age ideas, and there were several sweat lodges, caves, and Shamans. Trying Peyote is one of the reasons many people come here.

I had been told by a fellow backpacker, to be sure to go to the Magic Hostel in San Cristobal, as it was a terrific place to stay, and it was. The people staying there were all fascinating people, from Israel, Ireland, Denmark and Jamaica. Our international group all had to drink the local moonshine called *"posh"* it was horrid, almost like drinking kerosene, or at least the first drink was. It improved with a toast to each country represented there that night. There were some nasty hangovers the next day, and we all swore never to drink the local moonshine again.

Everyone who had consumed too much *posh* the night before decided we needed to try out one of the sweat lodges. The manager of our hostel owned a jeep, and offered to take us to his favorite spot.

We drove up into the hillside, alongside a beautiful, crystal clear creek. When we arrived at his chosen spot, we were greeted by several hill-side Indians. They led us down a trail to a rustic little hut made of overlapping palm branches. They started a bon-fire to heat the lodge, and then they all disappeared. One by one we would check the fire and the lodge, and talk about where all the people had gone. Finally, we agreed, it was time to sweat. The lodge was built beside a little river, so when it got too hot, a quick jump into the icy cold water was like pure heaven, and a sure cure for a hangover. When we finished our sweating, the people appeared again. They then led us up the mountain-side from the sweat lodge to the cave. Again these mysterious people disappeared. The cave's entrance was a small hole, but then became a huge room. We didn't venture in very deep, for fear of getting lost. I had done a bit of spelunking in the past, but always with someone who knew the cave, and this didn't seem like a good idea to me.

Returning to the sweat lodge, we were again greeted by several people, including a shaman. The shaman are normally hill-people, but I have no idea if he was a true shaman or not. He did a lot of ya-ya stuff over each of us, waving feathers and smoke over our bodies, and dancing wildly around each of us. He was exotic in his performance, and it was an exciting new adventure into a culture I knew nothing about. What did I experience from it? I think I discovered my funny-bone, because I laughed and laughed, in fact, I still laugh remembering it. Perhaps he was an amazing shaman, and gave me the gift of laughter..

As for peyote, well if you are ever in San Cristobal, it is easy to get, and highly recommended by the local shamans and all the back-packers.

It was time to leave this splendid little place, and I now had a couple of girls to travel with to Guatemala: Ann from London, and Hishomie from Japan. Hishomie only spoke Japanese, and was traveling alone to Guatemala to meet friends. She was only 16, or at least that was what I thought she told us, so Ann and I took her under our wings, as dubious as that may have been.

The three of us left San Cristobal at midnight for Tapachula, which was a seven-hour bus trip, but supposedly a better border crossing than the others. If Tapachula was the best border crossing, I'd hate to cross any of the others. It was horrid, with people yelling for our attention, men grabbing at us, and little boys trying to steal our backpacks. Immigration was not that cordial either, in fact, I had never seen so many people arguing with the officials.

Finally, we were through customs, and now we needed to change buses to Guatemala City. It is about a five-hour trip, and then one more hour to Antigua where we were all going for Spanish classes. The street men were all yelling that we needed to change our pesos to quetzals, but we ignored them. It was just too much of a madhouse to try to exchange money, and not be ripped off.

Once we got to Guatemala City, we found we actually did have to change money, as no one would accept Mexican pesos, or U.S. dollars. Having no Guatemalan money turned into a lot of walking, talking, and dickering for a favorable exchange rate. I thought it was a good idea to leave our packs with Hishomie while Ann and I went to find a money exchange. Ann wouldn't leave her stuff with anyone, as she had lost everything she owned by doing that somewhere before. So off we went with heavy packs, temperature in the 90s, and between us such little Spanish that the Guatemalans didn't recognize a word we spoke. I think we got ripped off pretty badly, but at least we had some *quetzals* (Guatemalan money) for the bus to Antigua.

I had read about "chicken buses" and that was certainly what our bus to Antigua was. Our packs were thrown on the top of the bus, to make room for more people, which was already fully packed. I would rename those buses "sardine" buses, as there were so many people you couldn't move. We stood for the entire hour with our arms raised and with someone else's arm pit in our face, or ours in their face. The noise was deafening with everyone playing their own music as loud as their radios would blast. If there were chickens on that bus, I'm sure they would all have been crushed before they got to the market.

Our first thing to do in Antigua was to make sure Hishomie found the hotel where her friends were staying. That worked out quickly and quite by accident. When we were walking towards her hotel her group from Japan just showed up on the street. It was fun to meet her friends, most of them spoke some English, so we finally could communicate with her. They all thanked us for looking after her, and off Ann and I went to find a room.

We decided on the Posada La Quinta since it looked like a decent little hotel with a good location. However, the next day it became somewhat weird. It seemed that the hotel changed into a church. We were told we needed to be very quiet from 6PM to 9PM, as there would be a religious service held in the lobby.

I was familiar with the Mexican Catholic church, and this service was definitely not Catholic. Looking down from the balcony, I watched as they assembled an extremely life-like manger. They had a ton of hay for the manager, and then a live burro and two baby lambs arrived. Mary and Joseph walked in with baby Jesus, thankfully, not a real child, but a life-sized doll. It all appeared quite traditional, rather like watching live-theater. Then I don't know what happened, but it got kicked up a notch. It was like watching a Broadway play called, "Baby Jesus Meets Kiss". Five or six men with huge feather-headdresses, and their bodies painted like animals came screaming in. They danced and yelled, grabbed up the doll and threw it around. Next came some men or women with black capes covering their heads. The feathered men took up spears and knives, as they danced and slashed at the hooded people. Shockingly, there appeared red stuff, like blood. This was done with lots of yelling, and wild dancing. Last came a man whose entire body was painted black. He spun and twirled, then like magic, he lit a small fire in his hand. When he grabbed up the doll everyone became silent. He seemed to pray over the doll, and then pass it over the fire and hand it to the next person. Each person did a repeat of this until the end of the line. Finally, the doll was placed back in the manager. For the next hour, it was as if they were each loudly praying in a strange language.

At this point, I had pushed far back on the balcony. At times, I felt like I was invading a private and personal religion, and shouldn't be a peeping-Tom, but I couldn't leave. When the fire was lit, I thought it was a good idea to know how to get out of there quickly, but that wouldn't be an option, because we would have to go through the lobby to get to the street. We decided if necessary we could climb out the bathroom window to the street. They had told us we had to be quiet, but I think that was so all the loud music, and people yelling could be heard ten miles away. It was the most unusual religious service I had ever witnessed. Later when I made friends in Antigua, I asked about this church. Everyone smiled and said, "It's just their way to celebrate Jesus."

Ann was leaving the next day, and I sure wasn't staying in the church/hotel alone. It was time for me to find a school and housing, as that is why I was in Antigua. After checking out several schools, I registered at Don Pedro Alvarado. This wasn't an easy decision because Antigua had over eighty Spanish language schools. It was just one of several that felt right to me, plus they would arrange room and board (a home stay) with a local family.

I thought the school was pretty decent, but maybe not as fancy as some other schools that my friends attended. I enrolled for three hours of classes, five days a week. I had a choice, whether to keep the same teacher or change weekly. My teachers spoke English, but it was not allowed in the school. So for three hours it was total Spanish. Then I returned to my home stay, where English was not allowed either, so it was Spanish everywhere, all day. There were times of great frustration, not knowing a needed word, or wanting to explain something in greater detail than my vocabulary allowed. But, slowly it became easier, and my brain and ears cooperated.

My home stay was certified by the government. Each home stay needs to be approved for adequate space, cleanliness, food service, and other strange little details. I think I had one of the best. The family I lived with were completely charming. Ruth the owner, had three delightful children whom I practiced my Spanish with, while they studied English. Ruth had a wicked sense of humor and told wonderful stories of her life. Ruth's husband was a lawyer in Guatemala City and came home only once while I was there. Ruth told me, "That's because his mistress doesn't like for him to see his family." She thought it was a good idea for him to stay in Guatemala City, because he was a government lawyer, and he'd had several death threats, so she was just as happy for him to stay with his mistress.

Antigua was an unusual Guatemalan city built in a beautiful valley with three volcanoes surrounding it. While I was there the one named Fuego erupted, and it was a breathtaking sight at night with the lava flowing down the side. I hiked Mt Agua, which was at least five-hours to the top, and then we couldn't even see much because of the low clouds hanging over the edge. The best part was that it only took about an hour and a half to get down. Why did I do it? Because I thought I could, and the guides said lots of people my age did it, but I also thought it was now or never. Was it worth it? Absolutely not! In my lifetime, I had already climbed many mountains just to get to the top, and this was not that much different, only it was a conquest to know that I had climbed a living breathing volcano.

With all the Spanish schools, Antigua had to be one of the richest cities in Guatemala. It is decidedly European, with elegant stores, and excessive prices. I'm not sure who was buying anything in these fancy shops as most people were young students, here to study Spanish. This city is known for its beautiful churches, and Easter processions. If Antigua was all you saw of Guatemala you would think it was a rich and elegant country, but it was the only rich city of its kind. The rest of Guatemala was dirt poor with many hungry people.

Our school had arranged for all of us to go to the kite festival in Santiago, a little village in the mountains. This annual festival was pure, true Guatemalan fun, much better than climbing a volcano. The kites were huge, ranging from ten to fifty feet long. They are made from bamboo poles and crepe paper. The festival was held on November 1st, the *Dia de los Muertos* (Day of the Dead) and the kites were all flown from the Santiago cemetery. The Day of the Dead is held in most Latin American countries with the belief that, for twenty-four-hours the spirits of loved ones return to earth. The local people believe the kites give the spirit's protection from other evil spirits. People from the village work for months creating their kites. The largest ones are only flown if the wind is adequate, and the spirits are ready to return.

As soon as someone thinks there is enough wind a kite will be lifted, and if all goes well more will soon join the flight. If the wind isn't sufficient the kite will quickly crash to the ground, and the month's work will be finished in a matter of seconds. Once several kites are in the air, the groups try to crash the other's kites, and the kite fights begin. It was an awesome sight, with hundreds of small and large kites filling the sky.

The school warned us to be extremely careful, as the best pickpockets in Guatemala would be there to try their skills. The crowds were so tight at times that anyone could pick a pocket. Several people on the bus back to Antigua reported they had been robbed. I thought it was sort of their own fault, because they thought they were smarter than the local robbers. Two people in our group foolishly had their credit cards in zip pockets on their legs, and they were gone. We were advised to be wary of small children, because they were some of the best at their trade. In the crowed streets, the kids could grab your leg or pocket, and who would think they would be lifting your wallet.

I had stopped before getting back on the bus to make sure I still had everything in my purse. However, as I was getting off the bus back in Antigua, I felt a hole in my purse. It had been cut down the side by a very sharp blade. Nothing was missing though, because I hadn't taken anything with me except water, a book, a pack of cigarettes, and a disposable camera. I think they felt sorry for me, so they left it all. How did this happen? A young woman with a baby, had sat down next to me on the bus, and asked me, if I would hold her baby for a minute. She then leaned over to talk to her friend, and I'm sure this is when she had cut my purse. It was somewhat spooky as those girls looked like sweet mamas with babies, and that knife had to have been really sharp; plus my hand was on my purse the entire time. I was sure it was the young girl with the baby because after I had held her baby they got off at the next stop, and they were the only ones who sat next to me for the whole trip.

Lesson 89 -- Beware of Mothers giving you their babies.

November 1st had another tradition in Guatemala besides Day of the Dead, and kites. It was a dish called *Fiambre*, and if you were lucky enough to eat it at someone's home, you were in for a real Guatemalan treat. Ruth, the owner of my home stay prepared this dish, and I was invited to watch her. *Fiambre* is meat, lots and lots of meat, sausage of all kinds like; chorizo, chorizo negro, sausage Americana, smoky links, plus chicken and pork all sliced thinly and also several different types of ham. Then she added lots of vegetables; carrots, cauliflower, broccoli, peas, fava beans and chilies. This was all marinated in vinegar and oil for two days. She then topped it with hard-boiled eggs and radish flowers. *Fiambre* wasn't that delicious at the restaurants, but Ruth's was super scrumptious. I promised to return next year, just to eat it once again.

Taking a short vacation from my Spanish class, I caught a bus to Honduras. Strange as it seemed, I ran into Paul at the border. Paul was one of my friends who had consumed too much *posh* (moonshine), and we had done the sweat lodge, caves, and Shamans, in San Cristobal together. Happy to see each other again, we had some fun stories to reminisce about. He was also going to Copan, so once again I had another lovely traveling companion and roommate.

We spent a couple of days at Copan touring the ruins and the little town. The ruins of Copan were again another emotional and spiritual day for me. The tunnels of Copan were an amazing sight, with ornate wall carvings, and intricate statues. The Mayans had built new temples on top of the old temples, and it was all there in front of my eyes. This was entirely different from the ruins I had seen in the past. The amount of butterflies alone in this area were worth the trip, and the Macaws were an added pleasure.

Paul was going diving at the Bay Islands, and I was going to Tela, so we caught the same bus from Copan to San Pedro Sula together. Before we got to the bus station on the highway, we were all loaded into the back of a pick-up truck, then onto a school bus, and finally we boarded a real air-conditioned bus. Everyone was laughing at all the transfers, but the nice thing about backpackers is they always find joy and humor in the moment, and this was one of those humorous moments.

At San Pedro Sula, we had to go from one bus terminal to another to get our correct bus. There was a large group of us all running to catch one bus or another. We didn't know each other, as we had all just gotten off different buses, but were all headed in one direction.

Paul and I were trying to get ahead of the group because we didn't know how many of these people wanted the same bus as we did.

San Pedro Sula was a city of a million people, so the streets were extremely busy; like all Central American cities, the vendors' stalls were right out onto the streets, making it difficult to run. As we all ran dodging vendor stalls, people shopping, and cars, my group stopped at one point, because there was a car revving its motor. We wondered if it was going to come at us, or go forward. Suddenly, it crashed into our group of people, hitting several of us. One of the guys cut his wrist on the rusty fender of the car, and blood was spraying everywhere. We were all pulling clothes from our packs, and trying to wrap his arm, calling for help. Another person had been knocked down and may have a broken leg. Finally, we heard the sirens and saw the flashing lights, to our relief help was on the way. It seemed it took forever for the ambulance to pass through the crowded street of people and cars.

After the ambulance arrived, Paul and I kept going towards the bus stop. Paul being a better runner than me, rushed ahead to buy our bus tickets. The car had hit my knee pretty hard, but I didn't think anything was wrong. Then as I was running to cross the street, my knee gave way. The pain was excruciating, and then I saw my knee was now on the side of my leg, not in the middle where it belonged. I thought I might pass out.

I remember seeing three guys sitting on the back of a truck, and all of them saying "OHHHH"! I was thinking, *I was going to go down, and if I did I was going to be run over by a hundred cars*. I had seen how little concern the people had for the blood, or the ambulance, so what was one more bloody, or dead person.

I somehow dropped my pack, doubled up my fists, and hit the side of my knee as hard as I could, and miraculously it went back in place! I think I'd seen Bruce Willis or some hunk do this in a movie. Wiping tears and sweat from my face, I looked over, and the three men were still watching, moaning, and yelling *"Bravo! Bravo!"* I was unsure for a few minutes if my breakfast was going to stay down, as my stomach was doing wild flip-flops. But, I sure didn't want to lose it, in front of my audience. So, I grabbed my pack and limped across the street to the bus station. It hurt like hell, but I thought it would hold me, and I'd make it to the bus stop, and catch the bus in time.

Paul kept asking if I was alright, and if I needed a doctor. He wasn't sure we should get on the bus, but I thought sitting might be a nice plan, and so we climbed aboard. At that point, I just knew I was happy to be able to keep my leg elevated on his lap, and to have someone care about my well being.

After sitting on the bus for a couple of hours, we arrived in Tela. Now the question was, could I walk? I quickly kissed Paul good-bye and hobbled off the bus. It had stopped at a gas station on the outskirts of town. The night was pitch black. The station was closed. There were no taxis. I felt my heartbeat go from normal to heart-attack rate. This was clearly a dangerous situation to have placed myself in. I couldn't believe how stupid I had been to get off that bus, and not keep going with Paul to the islands. I honestly had no idea what I was going to do, but I did know one thing for sure, I wasn't going to walk anywhere.

Then I noticed some people hanging around a big black car in the shadows of the station. That was all, just a black car, and some girls, obviously (professional ladies) getting into the car with the biggest black man I had ever seen. He was close to seven feet tall and weighed at least 300 pounds. I'm not that stupid, I knew he was their pimp, but I yelled to him anyway, *"Señor por favor, necesito su ayuda!"* (please, I need your help). This huge dude slowly comes over, and asks in perfect English what I needed. So I politely asked him, if he could give me a ride into town, and find me a hotel. I told him about my leg, and that I could seriously use some help with my pack and getting to his car.

He was so nice; he helped me walk, stumble, hobble to his car, and I piled in with the girls. Was I nervous or scared? No! I was in so much pain I didn't care what they did with me. My huge black guardian angel and the driver started to argue about where to take me, or so I thought, as my Spanish fails at times when they speak too fast. Whatever the disagreement was, I felt sure the big guy would come out the winner.

They decided to take me to Hotel Marisco. When we got to the hotel, my big old angel went in and got help. He told me, "No matter what, do not leave this hotel tonight. You will be safe here, and if you need anything they will go get it, but it is not safe outside at night for you here." I was quick to figure out that a white lady who couldn't even walk wouldn't be too safe, anywhere in the world alone on a dark street. I thanked these sweet people, and when I told the girls, "*Gracias, Señoritas*," they all giggled, and told me no one ever calls them ladies, then they each kissed me on both cheeks, and told me to be very careful.

The nice lady at the front desk helped me to my room, and later sent a darling little old man to my room to massage my leg. He sat and crushed aspirin into lime juice and massaged my knee with his concoction. My God it hurt, and he knew it. But he told me, he had to do it strong to help the pain. Then this darling little man brought me some beer, cigarettes, and his own personal radio.

The next morning he returned to massage my leg again, and by then I could walk a little better, so I headed to the pharmacy for some muscle relaxers. After explaining to them what I wanted and why, they all were insistent that I needed painkillers. Okay, but I also want muscle relaxers, too. I'm not sure what I got, but it was some really good stuff. In an hour, I was definitely feeling no pain.

Tela, had such a beautiful beach with perfect water, and yet I was afraid my leg wouldn't hold me if I were hit by a big wave. So I sat on the beach, ate incredible shrimp soup, and listened to young beach boys play their guitars, or flutes, and missed the inviting water.

After my experience with the Garifuna man and his ladies, I wanted to see their village. The Garifuna people are spread throughout the Caribbean, and their heritage is African. They are beautiful people with the longest legs I've ever seen. Their music, which was playing everywhere, was unquestionably upbeat, and their dancing was crazy, wild and free. I spent most of the day watching the men fish, and the women tending the children and making their famous cassava, or yucca bread. The women young and old, sat in a group visiting with me, all the while grating the cassava. When they had it as shredded, and as dry as they wanted, it was time to throw it in a hot pan, and quickly fry it. It was delicious with a little honey dripped on top.

Many of these people spoke Spanish, Garifuna, French, and English. It was surprising to hear so much English, though I thought it might have been for my benefit rather than their choice of language. Either way, it was helpful to me. They were all intrigued by my blonde hair and blue eyes, but most of all by the fact, that at my age, I was traveling alone. In fact, one of the girls insisted she needed to walk me back to Tela as she didn't want me to go alone. They all said, "Tela is a dangerous place and especially for a white woman alone." How dangerous can it be when a man will pick you up at the gas station in the middle of the night, take you to town for free, and make sure you were safe? And now she wanted to walk me to my hotel, so I would be safe. Wow! Tela, sure wasn't dangerous for me.

I had to return to San Pedro Sula to catch another bus back to Antigua, but this time, instead of running, I took a taxi. Well, two taxis, because the first one took me to the wrong bus terminal.

I returned to Antigua on November 11th, my fifty-ninth birthday. Ruth, the owner of my home stay had arranged a party for me, and it was a very nice surprise. I was excited to see Thomas and Dengue (our name for him) at my party, because before I left for Honduras, Dengue a young big strapping boy from Denmark, had gotten dengue fever. One day he was healthy, and two days later he was stooped over like an old man. His eyes were like flowing blood, and he was white as a sheet, and still had a high fever. He told us he had never been in such pain, with every bone in his body aching. I guess that is why they call it the "bone-cracking disease". He didn't know whether to return to Denmark, or stay where the doctors knew about dengue fever. I was glad to see he had improved by the day of my party, and that he wasn't in as much pain.

Thomas, Dengue (my friend, not the disease) and I used to go to this little bar, where they would drive the bartender nuts with their strange request for drinks. They taught me to hold this weird orange liquor in my mouth, and then they would light a match, and tell me to blow slowly out. At that moment, I was a fire-eater! Just utterly crazy, but so terribly funny that the bartender had to try it also. It became a hot seller at his bar. These guys also mixed vodka and Fishermen's Friend, a cough-drop, together. My friends loved it, but

I thought it was more like cough syrup than a good drink, and even the bartender agreed with me. It was gross. These two guys and I had a lot of fun together practicing our Spanish, drinking, and laughing at them try to capture the heart of the Guatemalan girls.

Those two young men and I still keep in touch, and Kathy from Germany (one of the people staying at my home-stay) left me a note under my door, the morning I left. This lovely note said, "I have never liked Americans because of what I had heard about them, but after knowing you, I have to change my mind about nasty Americans." I'm not telling you this to pat myself on the back, but to tell you; that when we travel we can change the world, or at the very least, one person's negative thoughts.

November 24th, I left Antigua on the chicken bus for Guatemala City to catch my flight to San Salvador and then on to Seattle.

I needed to go home because I was going to be a grandmother sometime in December. What could be more exciting than that? I had better get my knitting needles going, and practice how to secure a tiny diaper, once again. Oh man, this is going to be another exciting adventure.

After witnessing the birth of my grandson, I knew nothing could compare to that new adventure. But I still had the urge to travel, and both my daughters told me to keep going. I couldn't have done any of this without their support, so thanks to them, I was off to Thailand.

My friend Terry from Mexico had called and invited me to go to Thailand with her and another friend. Having spent the last three years traveling solo and loving it, I was a little apprehensive about joining them. Then Terry called again to let me know another woman would be joining us. That made four of us, and I only knew one of them. But I'd already bought my ticket and planned an escape route in case it didn't work out.

My ticket read Seattle, Vancouver, Taipei, Bangkok. After about fifteen hours, we landed at Chiang Kai-shek International Airport in the People's Republic of China. I remembered reading about Chiang Kai-shek and China in high school and being so frightened of them. Now I was there! That airport was the first photo I ever wanted to take, but there were signs everywhere saying, "No Photos Allowed." I thought that for once I'd better abide by the rules, but I sure ached for a photo of that airport sign.

I had a few hours to burn at the airport, so I went to see where I could smoke. If the smoking rooms in Asia don't kill you, nothing will. They were little enclosed rooms with yellow nicotine dripping down the walls and twenty or thirty Asian men puffing away, with only a small fan to clear the smoke. It was too nasty for me, and I quickly put out my cherished cigarette. I would wait until Bangkok for another one, which would be several more hours.

As I waited and waited for my backpack to arrive, I started to worry. I was kicking myself for not putting some clothes in my carry-on, at least my bathing suit. Now I had nothing. Everyone else began leaving, except for a few people who seemed extremely upset about their luggage. My backpack didn't arrive, so now I needed to fill out paperwork—more and more papers—until I felt a bit crazy for even bothering. If it were found, who would care, and how would they find me? However, the person responsible for lost luggage seemed to know what he was doing and was terrific at handling angry people. In Asia, it is not polite to express anger, which worked in my favor since it had all become an impossible joke to me, and I just kept smiling and nodding my head in agreement with him.

Terry, Sara, and Cathy were waiting when I opened the door from the baggage area. Terry was screaming with joy to see me, she'd been worried I hadn't made my flight. It was now around 2 AM, and we were to catch a flight to Phuket at 7 AM, so we decided to wait at the bar and get to know each other. We drank a bit, slept a little, and laughed a lot. I began to think it would work out to travel with them.

The next day, there I was at the beautiful beach in Phuket, Thailand, with no swimsuit. We all laughed when Terry said, "Don't worry. You can wear one of mine." Terry is maybe a 42DD, while I might be a 34B. We were still laughing as I proudly walked down the beach with my new, improved front, although I couldn't help worrying what might happen if a big wave hit me.

Phuket was everything I had read about—the beaches long stretches of white sand bordering perfectly blue water—with one small exception: lots and lots of jellyfish. They were so tiny, you couldn't see them, but after being in the water for a few minutes, the itching from their stings became unbearable. Those nasty buggers managed to get inside my swimsuit, making my boobs and butt so itchy I wanted to tear off my suit.

It became a fun pass time to watch and make bets as to how long it would be before someone started to scratch or leave the water with a strange look on their face.

Karon Beach, where we were staying in Phuket, was a quiet little spot, while Hat Patong, just over the hill, offered a wild nightlife filled with *farangs* (foreigners), all-night parties, and transvestites. Thailand is known for its ladyboys, and I think Phuket had more than anywhere else in Thailand. Some were so beautiful you would never guess they were men. They put on some top-notch shows, but on the street, these men/women became extremely aggressive, wanting payment even for looking at them. While I found them intriguing, they disgusted one of my traveling companions. She had a fit whenever one came close to her, or if we wanted to take a photo with them.

Hat Patong also had live music nightly, Thai performers singing English songs by the likes of Elvis, the Beatles, and Bob Marley to perfection. You'd never know it wasn't the real thing until you saw them. It was a night of sheer fun, the music, the laughter, and the street people making me feel we really were in crazy, wild Thailand.

We spent the next day with hundreds of other tourists visiting tourist traps like the monkey caves, gypsy islands, and the famous James Bond Island, which may have been a beautiful island once but was now filled with trinket-vendor shacks and so many groups of tourists you could hardly walk. I had never been on the tourist route before and hoped never to repeat it.

Wonders never cease! When we returned to our hotel, there sat my backpack! I hadn't believed I'd ever see it again, let alone in only two days. I was so happy to see my swimsuit and a couple of good books. I felt I'd won the lottery. After a dinner on the beach of the largest prawns I'd ever eaten (even bigger than the lobster we'd had there), we decided to see what nightlife Karon Beach had to offer.

Just down the street from our hotel, we had seen a large area with signs advertising dancing, famous transvestites, great food, and the best party on the island. As we entered this area of tents and booths, a girl at one of the booths yelled at Sara, "Hey, sexy fat girl, come here! You are so fat and so sexy." Although that is just the way they are in Thailand, not meaning to be discourteous, they are extremely vocal about appearance, especially someone's weight, we quickly departed for Sara's sake and stopped at the first place we found to have a drink.

As soon as we sat down, we realized that all the beautiful women there were "working girls" and not happy about having to serve us our measly beer. As we watched them perform their seduction on a few men, one of the lovely ladies picked a man's pocket. He was a tourist and seriously drunk, but his friend saw what happened and yelled for the police. Then there was a loud bang-bang-bang ... of firecrackers.

However, Cathy freaked out, thinking it was gunfire, dived under the table, crying hysterically. One of the working girls tried to help her, but this just scared her more. She was screaming, "Get me out of here! Get me out of here before they kill us all!" When the police showed up, they thought the problem was with us. While they were trying to get Cathy to calm down and tell them what happened, the man who needed their help was still yelling for help. And so ended our last night in Phuket.

The next day was much better. The ferry trip to Koh Phi Phi was perfect, sitting with the local Thai people, drinking beer, and laughing with other travelers. When we reached the island, we had to transfer quickly to a long-tail boat that would take us to a beach a few minutes away. We had room reservations in Long Beach on Koh Phi Phi Island, a sweet place with rustic little bungalows, a lovely, clean beach, incredible Thai food, and friendly people.

The long-tail boats, the subject of many of our photos, are standard Thai transportation between the islands Their propellers hang six to eight feet off the stern on a long drive shaft, allowing them into the shallowest of waters while still maintaining control. Taking the long-tail boats snorkeling, or to Phi Phi was a daily or nightly event for us.

Koh Phi Phi was an elegant island. It was different from most of the places we had seen, with lots of hippy backpackers, but the very rich also came to experience the island's beauty. You could walk at least a mile into the ocean before you were over your head, and the water was so clear you could see fish swimming by your legs. Despite being one of the most popular islands in Thailand, it never felt overcrowded. Being able to stay in Long Beach, a quiet little spot, and still go to Koh Phi Phi, with its action day and night, whenever we wanted was a perfect situation.

A few days later we took a two-hour ferry trip to Krabi, and then on to Surit Thani, then another bus, and finally a ferry to Koh Samui. This seems to be one of foreigners' favorite beaches. It is lined with fancy hotels, expensive restaurants, and of course a McDonald's, all decidedly Americanized. We had a lovely hotel with a pool and the beach directly in front, but we were there with hundreds of other tourists.

On our first night in Koh Samui, Terry met Lawrence from England. He was an adventurer and talked us all into renting an old army jeep, which gave us the freedom to see the entire island. And what a beautiful island it was, with waterfalls, colorful birds, and orchids everywhere—just the way I always imagined a jungle should look.

We hiked a small foot trail through the mountains to a river with more beautiful waterfalls and crystal clear pools filled with thousands of tiny fish. The only other people there were children from a village over the hill. It was a memorable moment, and I felt lucky to share this spot with them. I could tell they were a little nervous when we first arrived, but after seeing us splashing in the pools, they relaxed and joined us. We spent the afternoon with these kids, chasing little fish. This would be their dinner, and we became much more serious about catching as many as we could, but those kids were the best at their job.

Driving the back roads, we saw more Buddha statues than I dreamed could be on one island and visited monks who told our fortunes. Having your fortune told was a nice way to make a donation to them, so we did this as often as possible.

After a few days in Koh Sumi, we caught a flight to Bangkok. Lawrence came with us because he'd had his passport stolen and needed to go to immigration. We spent a couple of days having a wild time in the big city. We were staying on Khaosan Road, which is the hot spot for fun, fun, fun. We did every street market in the area, plus the night markets, and took the riverboat to the center of town, so the other girls could shop in some of the most elegant stores in the world. It was amazing how modern and expensive the central area of the city was.

We tried to see the Grand Palace, but they wouldn't let Terry in, saying she wasn't dressed appropriately, although she had on a long wrap skirt just like the rest of us. She couldn't understand what the problem was, so I explained what I thought was the problem. Extremely well endowed, no matter what she wore on top, the Buddhists wouldn't find it appropriate.

While the other girls saw the Grand Palace, Terry and I had our fortunes told by the oldest monk alive. He had to be at least one hundred years old He asked our day of birth, the time, and the location. He felt our hands and looked at them as if they were a detailed book. He even checked our ears, feeling and pulling them. After consulting a huge book, he went into great detail about our history and our future, much better than Psychic Hotline. I didn't care what he told me; I just loved being in his presence, gazing into his old eyes and withered face. I think I fell in love with that old monk!

Sadly, the time came for the other girls to leave Thailand. Although we were unsure how we would all get along when we started this trip, we had grown to accept, respect, and like each other, and it was an emotional goodbye.

Lawrence and I decided to stay and enjoy Bangkok for a few more days. Our hotel was just off famous Khaosan Road, a shopping street in the daytime and a party street at night, when traffic was blocked and the bars pulled their tables out onto the street, creating one big street bar.

Lawrence and I were sitting at one of the sidewalk tables when a woman with only one arm stopped and picked up his cigarette lighter, an old Zippo. She couldn't light it, but when I took it from her and tried to help, she grabbed it back, threw it at me, and started screaming. I didn't understand the language, but body language is the same the world over. All the Thai boys were laughing hysterically, but when I asked what she was saying, they told me, "She is just crazy." Her ranting went on for at least fifteen minutes, until a policeman came to see what was happening and took her a short distance away, but she continued pointing and screaming at me. I'd been told several times, "Those cigarettes are going to kill you." But that night I thought it might be a cigarette lighter instead.

Lesson 352: Never give help to those who think they don't need it.

When Lawrence went to immigration to get a new passport, I tagged along to see if I could renew my visa. They told me, I couldn't renew it there, that I needed to cross a border, and then I would be able to return to Thailand. Traveling to Cambodia's border sounded like a great idea, and Lawrence decided to join me for a few days. From Bangkok, our destination of Koh Chang took about eight hours, with a stop in Trat for the night, as there were no ferries to Koh Chang after 6 PM.

Trat appeared more like a normal Thai town, rather than just a tourist area. We spent the evening at an outdoor market, which was huge for such a small population, and had foods I'd never seen before in Thailand. After trying some of these, we found a cute bar filled with local people. The bar was especially intriguing that night because they were preparing food for a religious ceremony. The tables were filled with strange and very lovely looking dishes, which would be taken to the temple and placed on the steps or the altar to make the gods happy. Much later that night they would return to collect it, then it was served at a special family dinner the next day. This food was believed to have been blessed by the gods.

Later that night, the bartender offered me one of the fancy eggs. I peeled the decorations off and took a bite. Oh my God, it was the worst tasting thing imaginable. It was like biting into garbage from a dumpster. Even though, I was trying to be polite, I had to spit the horrid bite into a napkin, then drink and spit, drink and spit. I have eaten grasshoppers, cockroaches, ants, pig intestines, calf testicles, and cow eyeballs, but this was the worst. I hoped the gods didn't agree with me.

The next morning we caught the ferry for Koh Chang. On board were two young prostitutes with a couple of old German men. The girls were looking at Lawrence and me and laughing. I understood; they thought I had hired Lawrence as my boy-toy. When I told him what was going on, he insisted on putting on a show for them. The old Germans and the Thai girls seemed to enjoy his show, but I didn't think their show was entertaining at all. I detested seeing fat, old men with young Thai girls, so prevalent everywhere in Thailand.

Lawrence spent a few days in Koh Chang then left for Cambodia and onward to Laos. It had been fun having him around, but I wondered who he really was. He had lost his passport or had it stolen twice in two months, which seemed a little fishy.

I'd found a lovely spot in Koh Chang and stayed and stayed. There were white-sand beaches, crystal blue-green water, fantastic Thai and American food, first-run movies at night in several restaurants, a cheap, clean hotel room, and best of all, friendly, happy people. The only problem was that I had to renew my visa in ten days. I planned to go to Cambodia the next week with Sharon, a Canadian woman who was on vacation from teaching ESL in Korea. We intended to take a ferry to Trat, catch a bus to the border at Had Lek, get our passports stamped, do a week or so of traveling in Cambodia, and then return to Koh Chang.

The big news on the island the next day, was that the Cambodians had burned the Thailand embassy in Phnom Penh, the Cambodian capital. All borders were closed, and the Thai army was being called out to protect the frontier. This was the talk of the island, and it continued for several days. I still had a few days left on my visa, but I'd have to leave for Bangkok if the situation didn't change soon.

We had TV news coverage, but it was all in Thai, of course, so it had to be interpreted for us. On the fourth day, everyone agreed that the border had been opened. Sharon and I made plans to rent a jeep with a driver, since there weren't buses going there this week. No one was sure why the buses weren't operating, but they figured it was because no one wanted to cross the borders now. Most people from Thailand go to Cambodia to gamble or vacation, and the people in Thailand were still angry their embassy had been burned, so no one was traveling. Well, whether we wanted to go to Cambodia or not, we needed to, if we wanted our visas updated.

The next morning, our jeep and driver, Phan, a friend of Sharon's, arrived right on time. We loaded up and caught our ferry to Trat. Phan thought it would take us about three hours to the border. He said it was a busy crossing because so many people from Thailand went to Cambodia to gamble in their casinos, so we might have to wait in line for an hour or two. Phan agreed to wait for us, because we both decided against traveling in Cambodia until things settled down.

As we approached Had Lek, we saw no lines of people, just hundreds of empty stands that usually sold fruit, vegetables, or crafts. All the main stores were closed too. As Phan pulled up to immigration, he said, "Oh, my God, I don't think this is good. It is just too strange today. We need to go home, now." Sharon asked if I wanted to go back. My thought was that neither side was angry with either of us nor our countries, so we should just keep going and see how it worked out. I was a little nervous though, because Phan was white-knuckled and insisted it wasn't a good idea.

The Thai border guards knew why we were there, as many foreigners do this visa run. They quickly stamped our passports, opened the makeshift barbed wire gate, and told us to walk across the bridge to the Cambodian border. Normally there was a shuttle bus, but not today because no one was crossing the border—no one but the two of us.

We started walking, and as I looked back at the barbed wire blockade, I saw at least six Thai military men with machine guns pointed in our direction. My heart was pounding and my entire body covered in sweat, I thought this might be the stupidest thing I had ever done. I walked as fast as possible, believing Cambodia had to be better … if we didn't get shot first.

But as we quickly crossed this hellishly long bridge, I could see more machine-guns pointed at us from the Cambodian border. We kept going, neither of us saying a word, we had to go somewhere. And as we approached this ugly blockade, I saw that the Cambodian soldiers were smiling and nudging each other. The sentries from both countries looked maybe sixteen to eighteen years old, and I guessed this was a lot of fun for them, perhaps an exciting escape from their usual boring job. One thing in our favor was that we obviously weren't Thai, both of us being very white-skinned with blonde hair.

The friendly, smiling, young Cambodians stamped our passports and opened the horrid-looking gate once more. Then we had to walk that long, long bridge back to Thailand. I hoped none of them would think it might be fun to shoot us and throw us in the river. Who would ever know? Phan was the only person who knew where we were, and I thought he could be so scared he might just leave and quietly go home.

When we finally walked back into Thailand, with guns once again pointing at us. We presented our passports, which they pleasantly stamped. We both burst into hysterical laughter, hugging each other, and ran for a bathroom. Then at the one open store, we bought a bottle of Thai whiskey and Coke and had a much needed celebration.

Phan told us, he thought we were either very brave or terribly stupid, but he was now happy, and gave us both a huge hug. He said he had been very worried about us when he saw the guns. Later he asked us what he should have done if we hadn't returned. Neither Sharon nor I could give him a satisfactory answer, so we just made a joke about it all. The trip back to Koh Chang was pretty quiet.

After checking the Internet for teaching jobs in Thailand, I decided to go to Rayong. There were several ESL jobs there, plus it was on the ocean and close to Bangkok. It sounded like a good spot to live. I took the little ferry back to Trat and then a bus to Chontanburi. Once there, I needed to change to a funky, old school bus to Rayong. As we got close, I was already feeling it was an awful idea. This area was so ugly, with oil refineries blowing pollution everywhere. The guidebook neglected to say what a filthy, nasty place it was.

I knew I didn't want to spend even one night there. Wondering how to change plans, I threw my pack down, and lit a cigarette to help me think. I began eavesdropping on an English-speaking couple behind me, who seemed to feel the same. The woman was Thai, so I thought she should know what she was talking about. I finally confessed to them that I had been listening to their conversation, and they invited me to share a *songthaew* (a small truck with benches) to a beach the woman knew. Since it was about twenty kilometers from Rayong, I figured the air had to be better.

This was a lovely spot. There were no foreigners, only Thai people, and the beach to my joy, was covered with shells. I spent the days picking up shells with the locals, which surprised them, but they loved it. When the tide was out, we collected little pink ones for necklaces. I donated mine to the older ladies or the beach kids, which delighted everyone. When the tide came in, we would dig for tiny clams that the local people made into soup. I gave mine to the bar where I had been sitting, hoping to try these itty bitty clams.

A young girl named Kik was excited to meet me. She spoke a little English, and her brother had told her to come to the beach because there was a white woman speaking English, picking shells, and giving them to everyone. Kik and I picked shells together and talked, and soon mothers were bringing their little kids to listen to the foreign lady speaking English.

Later, Kik, along with a friend who played the guitar, met me at the beach and she gave me a little copper Singha dragon. It was a thoughtful gift because she knew I liked Singha beer, which has a dragon on its can. She explained that this would remind me forever of our day together on the beach. We had a great time drinking, dancing, and laughing with little English between us all.

I decided I'd travel by bus back to Phuket. Buses in Thailand are clean, air-conditioned, and go everywhere, even to remote areas. This way I could stop wherever I wanted and see the countryside. So I left dirty, polluted Rayong for Bangkok.

There are so many bus stations in Bangkok, that it was a nightmare getting to the correct one, going south. My first destination from Bangkok was Hau Hin, but getting there from Rayong took twelve hours. A lot of that time was spent in taxis taking me to the wrong stations. They all acted like they knew what they were doing, and I guess they did; it was called screwing over dumb tourists.

Lessons 446: Never leave it to a taxi driver to know where you truly want to go; figure it out yourself.

After the long and crappy day from one taxi to another, and then sitting on several buses, all I wanted was a bed. That didn't turn out to be as easy as I would have thought. There was a government meeting going on in Hau Hin, and rooms were at a premium. Finally, I found one and crashed for the night.

The next morning, I looked for a different room, and was lucky to find one at half what I paid the night before. It was a small hotel built over the water, sounds cool, right? It had a slight drawback, when the tide came in, so did the crabs, hundreds and hundreds of them. There weren't any crabs in my room, but the deck was covered and the walls moved with them. It was rather creepy but also entertaining. I love crab: to catch and to eat them, I even have a tattoo of one. But these were more like spiders, and these nasty, little critters were everywhere.

The beach at Hau Hin was shockingly filthy, with plastic everywhere, and an oil slick covering the water. I was glad to have a pleasant deck to lounge on at my hotel. I meet some fabulous people on our little deck that afternoon, one of them being a yummy singer from Ireland. He knew every song from the 60s to the 80s, and we all spent the afternoon drinking and listening to our own private show. I hated to leave the wonderful music and romantic man, but I had a night bus ticket to Phuket. Damn, I still kick myself for leaving that troubadour man. He could sure strum a guitar, and certainly knew how to play to an old lady's heart.

My night ride was one strange and uncomfortable trip. When I boarded the bus I had a reserved seat, but then I traded it with a couple of girls from Germany, so they could sit together. That was a huge mistake! I was then sitting with a boy from Israel, a cute, young, and not so nice boy. About fifteen minutes into the trip, he was holding my hand, and shortly there after, he was squeezing my leg. The seats were so close together that no matter what, we were snuggling with each other. For a short while, I thought it was pretty funny, but enough was enough, and quite soon I was getting a little tired of his stupidity. Finally, I told him to cut the crap; we could either ride together for twelve hours, or I could have his ass thrown off the bus. He laughed and kissed me. I couldn't believe this craziness, but the German girls were laughing and thinking it was incredibly funny. I threatened the girls to take back my original seat from them, or throw him over onto them. I kept telling him, "My God, I'm a grandmother; do you really want to do this to a grandmother?" Ha, ha, ha. He and the girls thought this was hilarious. Maybe that is why I get into screwy situations; because of my sense of humor and thinking life is to enjoy. I also thought he was pretty funny, in a bizarre sort of way, and it was hard to be stern. Soon we were all laughing about his craziness, and he finally shaped up, and took a nap. I had been warned about night buses, but this wasn't what the warnings were about!

When we stopped somewhere in the middle of the night, this naughty boy departed for places I hoped I wasn't going, and the girls from Germany and I went on to Phuket in peace.

Having been in Phuket a month before, I wasn't as naïve as usual. When the taxi driver insisted on taking me to his favorite, expensive hotels, I declined his recommendations. Once in the area I was familiar with, I asked to be let me off on the street corner. I easily found a room that was passable ... or so I thought. After spending a couple of days there, I woke up one morning to find I had no running water in my room. The boy from the kitchen brought me a bucket of water to bathe with and told me we wouldn't have water for several days. I decided I needed to find another room.

I ended up being glad my first hotel didn't have water, because I now had a terrific room with an air conditioner, TV, and water for the same price. Plus, the kids that ran it were incredibly crazy. There was a computer area and a beauty salon in the lobby, which was the gathering spot for lots of young Thais. Fam, the manager of the hotel/beauty-salon/computer center, was a gay hairstylist and a sweet young man. As I'm a former hairstylist, we had crazy fun together. I would color his hair every day in some wild, red, purple, or green color and spike it like a rock star. We would spend the morning laughing, doing his hair, drinking coffee, and talking. Fam would threaten his clients with haircuts like mine, which to them was shockingly short, but they all wanted him to bleach their hair my color.

One morning there was a peace march in Bangkok and Phuket. Fam told me he didn't think I should go out because I was an American. He was a little worried because a peace march in Thailand wasn't always peaceful. We spent the day playing cards, and then everyone agreed I could go out on our street because the people all knew me. The first thing I did was head for my favorite food stall.

I normally ate at the same street stalls, because they knew me and treated me so well, plus they had the best food. They called me Pad Thai because that was what I always ordered. After enjoying my pad thai, I would cross the street for a final treat of chicken hearts on a stick. I guess I was lucky they didn't name me Chicken Heart.

One night, the lady at the pad thai stand told me, "No more pad thai. You try curry chicken today. You like, it very good." She was right; it was very good. The next day I ordered pad thai again, and she laughed and said, "Sorry, no more pad thai. You try my secret Thai dish. It give you big breasts!" It was also exceptionally good, but I think she left out her secret ingredient, as nothing changed breast-wise.

Because of the heat, I never wear a bra unless I'm teaching. I hadn't given it much thought, but the ladies on my street in Phuket were all always interested in the old American without a bra. Many women on my street grabbed, touched, and shook my boobs. They even talked about them. These were women I saw every day, and we knew each other. They never did this to be sexual; it was all in fun. But I was curious why they were so interested in them. Their tops were usually very low cut, showing a lot of cleavage, and much more risqué than no bra. No matter the reason, it tickled my funny-bone, and theirs, so no harm was done.

At my hotel, Mimi, a sweet, young Thai girl, was in love with me. Whenever I came into the lobby, someone would yell, "Mimi! Come, Mimi! Donna is here!" Then Mimi would come running and profess her love to me. Several times I told her, "No, Mimi, no. I am not interested. I like men, not women. I'm sorry." One day it was just too much for her, and she started to cry. So I hugged her, which made everyone in the neighborhood happy because Pad Thai now loved Mimi. Mimi's love for me lasted the entire time I was there, and she never gave up on the idea of me loving her. I think it gave everyone on our street some extra fun, and good gossip. I'm sure it was more strange to me than it was to the local neighborhood.

Next door to my hotel was a travel agency, and the lady there wanted to perfect her English. So daily, my little group (the people from the street, and the hotel, or anyone walking by) and I would sit with her outside her business and practice English. Some days there were twenty or more people listening to us, and later you could hear them practicing with each other at their street stands.

I had given some thought to teaching in Thailand, but the pay was so meager, that I decided not to bother. I was just on vacation, and enjoying helping these wonderful street people. I know it was much more fun than dressing for class each day, doing lesson plans, or attending school meetings. I felt so rewarded and such love, that this time was to be valued.

I had my student, the travel agent, book me a ticket back to the United States, so the whole neighborhood knew I was leaving. The kids at my hotel spent the day cooking, and the people from the street booths all brought my favorite dishes, and we had one of the best parties I've ever attended. We laughed, cried, drank, and danced. Our street was shut down by the vendors pulling their stalls across the walk-way. As the night progressed, everyone's family arrived and it became a big block party. Many of these people I didn't know, but only for a few minutes, then we were all celebrating something.

It was a sad day when I said good-bye to my street friends. Fam, Mimi and Chicken-man, went with me to the airport. I wasn't sure what people at the airport thought when we walked in, and everyone was crying. I can say no one cries as loud as the Thai people. It drew lots of looks, but my heart was so full that I paid little concern to others. Then Fam started laughing, and there was no better sound. Everything was right with our world as I climbed aboard my flight back to the U.S.A., and all I could do was smile.

When I got back to the United States, my perfect world went to hell quicker than I could believe. My daughter Ginny had thyroid cancer, and I was more scared and angrier than I had ever been. One day we were all happy, carefree people, and the next day she was at the doctor's. And the next day they were sending her for emergency surgery. This is my baby and she had a baby only a few months old. This is a mother's worst nightmare.

Today my incredible daughter and her children are happy and healthy. So once again my world is beautiful, and I'm grateful to the Universe.

Lesson 1---Be thankful for what you have today.

CHAPTER 11

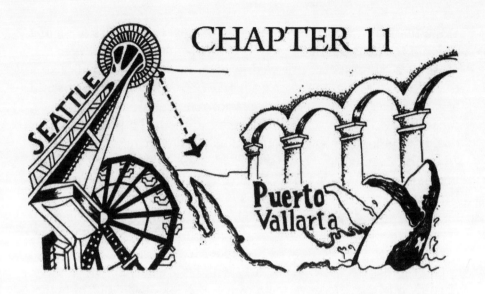

I tried to make a good decision about what to do after my daughter's recovery. I was still extremely worried about her health, so what I should do next weighed heavily on my mind. I knew I couldn't just stay there and watch over her, but I didn't want to go too far away. I decided on Mexico, which seemed to be where I went if I was in doubt as to what to do next, and I knew that if I were needed, I could get back to my daughter within a day. So back I went to Puerto Vallarta.

One positive thing about returning to a place you've already been; is it's so much easier than the unknown. Even the airport was familiar. And a lady from PV I'd met on the plane asked if I wanted a ride to town. She took me to the Hotel Hortencia, where I already knew the owners, and even got a discount on my room because they knew I was a teacher. I felt like I'd just come home.

I didn't have to worry about renting an apartment, as one was available right across the street. I arranged to meet the owner, and he was just the cutest little old man. The apartment was a delight, with a huge kitchen, a nice bathroom, and the living room/bedroom was okay, but he had a few things he needed to do before I moved in.

Señor Chuey, my new landlord, was 80 years old. His wife didn't live with him anymore; she lived in Guadalajara with their daughter. Señor Chuey instead had a mistress and a girlfriend. I learned this all in the first hour, while he was pouring me glass after glass of tequila and telling me he didn't like to rent to Mexicans, drunken *gringos*, or prostitutes. He insisted, I needed to learn to drink my tequila like a true Mexican, straight up with a squeeze of lemon and a lick of salt. I began to question his thoughts on not renting to drunken *gringos*, because I was sure that was happening to me as he poured another one. I fell in love with this funny old man, immediately.

He also wanted to know if I liked cats. Unsure why that was important. My answer was, "Not really." That was good, since he sometimes shot at them with his slingshot because they climbed in his windows and "pissed on his bed." By that time, I was holding my stomach from laughing so hard. I could tell he loved to entertain, which he proceeded to do with his great Mexican stories.

Later in the week, he had a party with his friends, all young guys, plus his mistress. He gave them orders that they were not to bother me, or as he said, "No hanky-panky with the teacher." He wanted me to meet all of them, in case they jumped over the fence at night. I was not to be afraid of them, and if he weren't there I should call one of them if I needed help. They all gave me their telephone numbers and email addresses.

One of them left me a note saying that if I needed or wanted him anytime day or night, he would be waiting, forever, outside my gate. Chuey told me, "Never believe anything they say, because they are all liars, very, very bad men, and they all have big mean wives."

Then they all laughed and told me, "No, no, Chuey is a liar, we don't have wives." Later I learned that they indeed were all married, were all liars, were all bad boys, and certainly could drink and laugh more than most people.

It was a good thing I had met all of them because on several nights, I heard a crash, bang, and lots of laughter, and knew it was his drunken friends climbing over the fence, to sleep at Chuey's instead of going home to an irate wife.

Señor Chuey told me he had eight kids, but he only liked one son and one daughter. He was sure the rest of them just came to see him when they thought he was ready to die. They will be extraordinarily wealthy when he dies, because he still owns prime property in downtown PV. He hadn't decided yet if he would leave them anything. Out of the closet came the tequila again, so I knew this was going to be another good story.

Many years ago, before Vallarta became popular with the *gringos*, Señor Chuey was the original owner of a well-known hotel on the beach. He and a partner had bought it when they were young men, but the partner got into financial problems and in came the Mexican Mafia to bail his partner out. Chuey didn't know about any of this until he started to get threatening notes about his need to sell the property. Then it got worse. They were threatening his family with death if he didn't sell his hotel to them. He sent his wife and children out of town and tried to deal with them on his own, with a little help from friends and some extra guns, but this didn't scare off the mafia.

One time he was thrown into the trunk of a car and left there all night and the following day. When he got out, he was almost dead from the heat and lack of water. At that point, he decided it was the end. He sold to those big, well-known corporate men and watched through the years as his little hotel became an enormous condominium building worth millions of dollars. He still owns some prime property, but not on the beach or worth millions.

This delightful little old man went to Cuba with his group of naughty young friends, but told me that I shouldn't go there because it had been too tough for them. He said, "We got cheated everywhere we went, and it was because we were Mexicans, and not respected by the Cubans. And you are a *gringa*! They will just rob you blind. But they will love your blonde hair, and blue eyes."

It was only my first week back, and I was all set with an apartment and a splendid old man with a wonderful line of bull. I had also found a small restaurant near my apartment, called Tia's, with fantastic Mexican food, and the owner wanted English lessons for her staff. We talked about times, prices, who, and where, then she paid me in advance for three days of lessons for three students, which is unheard of in Mexico. Usually it is quite difficult to get paid; it is always "I pay you *mañana*."

The next day, Jorge, a waiter from her restaurant, showed up for a class. He was from Argentina, a cute boy with a terrible scar down one side of his face. When I asked about it, he told me he had a bad knife fight with a gang in his hometown when he was a kid. We practiced restaurant language, and then he showed me a wallet photo of his father. Next, he wanted to go buy a bottle of water, and when he returned, he again took out his wallet, and out fell a condom. What did he think this class was, English and sex? I just ignored this and hoped he would get the message.

This same boy returned a week later, with a sad story to tell. He had lost his job because he had gotten into a fight with the cook, and he had also lost his apartment because he had gotten in a knife fight with his roommate. Now he would like to live with me. No! No! And no, he couldn't leave his pack with me: I knew he would come back for it late at night, and it would be hard to get rid of him. I understood how some of those Latino boys worked, and it was not going to work with me. This was one crazy boy, but I wished him well and told him not to come back, not tonight, and not ever.

We had started the rainy season in Vallarta. This could be a breath of fresh air, or just make it so humid you think you'll die. The ocean was dirty, and the rivers were full, but I had found a nice, clean swimming pool instead, and that was where I hung out during the day. The 180 bar/restaurant was a delightful place owned by a couple of Canadian women, but frequented by mainly local Mexican families, and a handful of *gringos*. On Sundays, they had live music, and it got a little wild at times.

One Sunday a super-drunk *gringa*, was telling everyone how she had lost more than a hundred pounds last year. Then she decided to show everyone her new body. Off came the bathing suit, and into the pool, she jumped. However, she must have forgotten she couldn't swim, or maybe she was just too drunk. She kept going down, and everyone was telling everyone else that someone should go help her. Eventually, the owners Barbara and Barbara, told the bartender, "You have to save her."

He whined to his bosses, "No! No! I can't do it. Have you seen her? I can't touch her! Just get the pole, and I'll pull her in." When she was finally pulled out of the pool, the bar was empty. I guess she did that more than once, and if she were there and drinking, no one ventured into the bar.

I was exceptionally lucky on one of those Sundays to meet a *señora* from Mexico City. Even at her age—I guessed, she might be in her eighties—she was a beautiful and elegant lady. Being the oldest people there, we struck up a conversation. Later, after a little tequila, she told me about her times with Diego Rivera and Frida Kahlo. Although I was sure she had told her story many times to many different people, I was pleased, she was sharing it with me.

She told me, "Diego loved women, and he loved me and loved me very well." She was sure that Frida had hated her and told lies about her to all her friends. She also thought that Frida had had more women lovers than men, but that she actually loved herself more than anyone. She said, "Frida was a very mean and selfish woman."

I enjoyed the afternoon with this fascinating lady, and she was thrilled that I was teaching English in Vallarta. We were to meet again, but she became very ill, and I never had another opportunity to visit with her.

This same restaurant was where "Dog," the bounty hunter, first sighted Andrew Luster. Andrew Luster, the heir to Max Factor, was an international fugitive on the run in Mexico in 2003. I wasn't at 180 when it happened, but the Sunday before, Luster had been there, and so were my daughter and I. We both remembered him because we had commented on the weird guy and moved away from him because he was just too creepy.

The bartender, Carlos, was the only one who talked with him. Carlos said that Luster wanted girls and cocaine, but Carlos told him he had to go to the bar around the corner to find those. That was funny because Carlos could get anything you wanted in about five minutes if he liked you. Carlos felt like all of us and said, "Luster was just too strange. I didn't want my girls with him."

Andrew Luster's arrest in Puerto Vallarta was the hot story in town for weeks, and it seemed to get bigger and wilder as time went by. The true story was that Luster had been accused of several counts of rape in the USA. While on trial, he left for Mexico and was declared a fugitive. His trial continued in his absence, and he was found guilty of eighty-six counts of rape. He was then captured, sent back to the USA, and sentenced to 124 years in the California prison system. "Dog" was subsequently arrested for deprivation of liberty, because bounty-hunting is illegal in Mexico, the charge ultimately dropped in 2007.

The entrance to my patio had a metal gate with sharp spikes on top, which kept us all safe from the local bad guys. Chuey had repeatedly told me to make sure I locked the gate because we lived on a busy street. I usually did lock it, but one day I was going in and out and forgot. I was busy mopping my floor that morning when I smelled a terrible stench. As I was smelling, mopping, and smelling, I looked up, and in my front doorway stood a very, very dirty, awful man.

I yelled at him, "Get the hell out of my house!" I could tell the man was so stoned he didn't know where he was, or what he was doing. And then he was in the doorway moving closer to me. But, I had an island between the door and my kitchen, so I felt pretty safe, so far. I thought if worse comes to worst, and he tried to come into the kitchen, I could jump over the counter, and run out the door.

All this time I was yelling for Chuey, and I could hear him running around upstairs, from room to room, but I knew it would take him forever to get down-stairs. I had my mop, but I didn't think this was a very reliable weapon. I grabbed a butcher knife, and I started shoving the knife at the smelly man, telling him if he didn't leave I'd cut his guts out. I knew he didn't speak English, but I couldn't think of the Spanish word for guts at that moment, so I was just poking the knife at him, and telling him *"Corte, corte, corte"*! (cut, cut, cut) My biggest concern was that I did not want that man to touch me, or anything in my house. He was the worst smelling thing I have ever encountered. I was still screaming for Chuey.

The smelly man was coming around the corner of the kitchen when in charged my friend Ivan from the Hotel Hortencia. Ivan is a huge Mexican, six feet tall and maybe three hundred pounds, and he was enough to get the smelly man's attention. Ivan grabbed him, and took him out to the street, and with a kick to the butt, told him to get the hell out of our area.

About that time, Chuey got down the stairs, to see what I was yelling about. He apologized and apologized for not getting there sooner, but his excuse was that he couldn't find his shoes; and he knew whatever the problem was, he needed his shoes. Both Ivan and Chuey lectured me on locking the gate, until my ears burned. I promised I would always lock that sucker, every single time. Then I went back inside and rewashed everything, as my house still smelled of my unwanted visitor.

I usually was better about locking that gate, because at 6 PM every night the *lengua* (tongue) taco stand opened directly in front of my patio, and people lined up at the gate. My diet was tacos, tacos, tacos. I could never pass up the one in front of my gate. When they were open the smell in my apartment made my mouth water, and I had to have one. I believe my neighborhood had the best choice for tacos in all of Vallarta. I had my *lengua* taco stand, then a few feet away a fantastic *birria* (goat) taco stand, and around the corner a *camarón* (shrimp) taco stand. I don't know if I was lucky or unlucky to have them all right in front of my nose. I did know for the first time in my life, I was getting some serious junk in the trunk (a fat butt). I guess that was okay thou as most Mexican men like a girl with a little meat on her bones, or so they say.

I started teaching at USA school with three hours in the morning and two hours from 4-6 PM, which was a perfect schedule for me. USA wasn't an elegant school for rich people. It was a school, subsidized by the government, to help less-advantaged Mexican families. José Antonio, the owner of USA, required students to submit a financial statement, with the cost of classes being determined by their income, and the need for English classes, on a sliding scale. Then they were tested in Spanish and English for placement into the correct level. Our student's ages ranged from 6 to 68 years old, and we had beginners to advanced students. Many foreigners living in Vallarta donated money to USA, and several of our students were on scholarships from their local schools.

With five hours of teaching a day, I could get by on my salary, but barely. It was much more than the Mexican teachers made, but still not much money. I tried to live like the Mexicans on my wages, but it was just not enough money for my lifestyle. I know I paid more for rent than the Mexican teachers, but I also live alone, not cutting the cost with others. My food was probably more expensive than theirs because I ate so many tacos, and not as much beans and rice as they did. However, the biggest difference was; that I smoked, and cigarettes weren't cheap, plus I loved to have a couple of beers on the beach, and that wasn't cheap either. However, I certainly wasn't living in the high-life either. My life was very simple; teach in the morning, later the beach, and teach again in the afternoon, then a little television and bed. But, still my money was gone before the end of the month.

So entered Victor into my life. Victor was a time-share salesman (one of those dreaded men on the streets of Mexico, who tries to lure foreigners into going to visit a new hotel or buy a vacation property). He was excellent at his job. He convinced me that this was an easy way to make a hundred dollars. He had me going to see time-shares, or vacation packages every free minute I had. I made $100USD for going to each one of those damnable presentations. He told me, "You make one hundred, and I make one hundred." What a bunch of bull! He made $400USD every time I went to see one and stayed for ninety minutes, and it usually took me three hours, not ninety minutes, to get out with my life.

If you have ever gone to a time-share presentation, you know how awful they can be. Why was I doing this? I swear Victor could sell ice to the Eskimos. Every time he'd tell me, "It's easy! You just make it more difficult than it is. Just go eat your breakfast, listen to them try to sell you a condo, or vacation package. Then tell them you didn't like something, leave, and collect one hundred dollars." Plus he always had a sad story to tell me, and I was suckered back into one more time to help him with his latest financial problem.

Every time we met I told him, "Victor, this is my last one."

His reply was always the same; "Oh, you little mother-flower, you know I'll see you again." Mother-flower was his favorite word, and I thought it sure beat Mother-fxxxer. It also became my favorite word when I was upset, excited or whenever needed, and it always made me laugh.

Victor did recruit some private students for me, and that helped a little, financially. One of these students was a young girl from the nearby small town of Bucerias. She traveled one hour each way for her lessons and always brought her grandmother with her. I only charged for one student, as they were both so sweet, and I knew they didn't have much money. Grandma was insistent that her granddaughter learned English, so she could have a better life.

Grandma was probably seventy-five, or older, and still she wanted to learn English. When they finished class, Grandma would kiss my cheeks, and say, "Thank you, oh, thank you teacher, thank you." That was why I loved what I was doing; the people were all so appreciative.

My next-door neighbor also found me another private student. She explained that the five-year-old boy was her boss's son, and his parents would pay me exceptionally well. I wasn't hot for teaching a little kid, and much preferring teens and adults. However, I went to the interview, and they offered me so much money (for Mexico) that I had to take it.

I was first interviewed by the mother, and then by the father. This was getting quite serious, as they were one of the wealthiest families in PV, though I didn't know that until I heard their last name. Then I got a little more excited because if it all went well I might get more students with their recommendations.

They both stressed that I needed to teach Roberto to read English in four months. They were moving to Florida, and he would be testing to enter the best kindergarten in the state. They told me, "This school is like the Harvard of kindergartens; he must get in with high marks." The father offered me the job and told me, that if Roberto passed his exam, I would be highly rewarded.

Finally, I was introduced to Roberto. His parents had told me earlier that the determining factor for being hired was; if I met Roberto's approval. He was extremely polite and mature, showing me his bed-room, the game-room, and then we went to see his dogs. He spoke beautiful English and Spanish, for a five year old. I was totally impressed, but then the attitude he had with the staff (what he called, "the servant") was shocking. I thought that would be our first lesson; how to be polite and thankful. I also wondered what I had stepped into!

Roberto, being five, really wasn't into anything other than playing, so I tried to make his lessons a game. I became his playmate/teacher. Did it work? Yes! Roberto was reading beyond level 1 in four months, and treating the staff (servants) much nicer. Did Roberto pass his exam at "Harvard's kindergarten"? Yes! Was I highly rewarded? No! They sort of forgot that part.

Once again I was leaving Mexico, friends, and students, but it was time to return to see my daughters and grandson. I couldn't wait to see my grandson Riley, and I hoped that he remembered me. It's funny how important grandchildren become in such a short time, but they do. No, I haven't become one of those grandmothers with her photo album in your face. I just keep him in my heart and his photos on my wall.

CHAPTER 12

When I told people I was going to Ho Chi Minh City, Vietnam, some asked, "Why?" Others asked, "Is it safe?" And a few people were openly disgusted. Some said, "Don't you know we fought a long and protracted war with Vietnam?" Yes, I remembered the war, and that was why I was going. I didn't really know how safe it would be, or what to expect. I just knew I wanted to go. The reason I wanted to teach ESL was to help other less fortunate people to have a better life. I had read about the destruction of the war, and I honestly wanted to be a part of creating a change in this war-torn country. Plus, I wanted to see Vietnam with my own eyes.

By some fluke, I read an advertisement in a Seattle newspaper for an ESL teaching job in Ho Chi Minh City (Saigon). I interviewed for it with a young man from ELS International, and the wife of the Vietnam school's director. They thought I would do well in Vietnam, and having already taught in Mexico certainly helped. They hired me that day, but they didn't know how long it would be before I received my contract from ELS in Vietnam. When my contract still hadn't arrived a few weeks later, I decided to go anyway.

I admit it was a bit foolhardy, and in reality, I didn't know what I would do if the job didn't materialize. I had plenty of time to think about that though, with twenty-four hours onboard EVA airlines. The excitement of the Orient began with an enforced stopover in

Taipei, Taiwan, Peoples Republic of China, where a typhoon closed the runway.

We were the last flight in, and our plane was full of nervous people. When you're in a foreign country and your airline wants you to give them your passport, that is a good time to get nervous. Anyone will tell you never to give up your passport, no matter what. Our airline took everyone's passport, and in return gave each of us a little piece of paper with a number on it. They herded us onto a bus and told us they were taking us to a hotel. That they did, and it was a very nice one, the five-star Chuto Plaza in Taoyuan City. Our rooms were elegant, and the restaurant was fantastic. We had a buffet of duck, crab, clams, snails, lobster, steak, and some incredible food I didn't recognize, plus anything we wanted to drink. I had green beer, green in color like green, green grass, freshly brewed and strangely delicious.

The next morning everyone was given breakfast and loaded back on the bus. The airport was a total madhouse. We were escorted to a huge room, and they started giving out passports. People were pushing and shoving, and it was getting a bit crazy. Finally, one man from Eva Airline took charge, and told us that the plane to Vietnam would not leave until everyone had received their passport, so not to worry.

I was lucky to have struck up a friendship with a *Viet Kieu* (a Vietnamese, who has lived in a foreign country), and he seemed more nervous about me being alone in his country alone, than I was. I was too excited to be worried, but he made sure I had his family's contact numbers should I need them.

A small group of us had sort of watched over each other during all the confusion in Taiwan. Among our group of new friends was a young Vietnamese couple from Canada going back to be married in their birthplace. The bride had her wedding gown as a carry-on, and it never left her sight. She said, this was the most indispensable item she possessed, and she would guard it with her life. Also in the group was my *Viet Kieu* friend, and a young Vietnamese boy from Seattle, who didn't speak a word of Vietnamese, because he had been raised in the U.S. and was going to meet his cousins for the first time. It was an emotional moment when we knew we wouldn't see each other again. It's incredible how quickly one makes friends when traveling together. My first introduction to the Vietnamese people was full of happiness and love, and I thought if the people in Vietnam were half as lovely as the people I had traveled with, it had to be a great country.

As we started our descent into Saigon, I could see many brown rivers against green, green fields of what I imagined being rice fields. I even saw a piece of the mighty Mekong. I was so excited! It was as if I had waited a lifetime to see this beautiful picture below me.

From reading and re-reading my trusty guidebook, I had chosen to stay at Hotel 64. The taxi driver kept telling me they would not have any rooms. It was too expensive, and it was not a good choice. He was insistent that he could take me to a better hotel, and it would be cheaper. I'm not sure why, but I was determined to stay at Hotel 64, no matter what he told me.

When I arrived, Madam Cuc met me at the door, and told me, "I'm sorry, no room tonight, my cousin will take you to her hotel, and then you come back tomorrow." A little bit of a girl threw my huge backpack on her scooter, and told me to get on, and off we went into the screaming traffic of Saigon. The next morning, this same little girl was back to pick me up, and return me to Madam Cuc's Hotel 64. This became my home for several months, and Madam Cuc and her staff became my family.

I had come to Saigon to live and teach, but I thought that before I accepted the contract at American Pacific University, I would check out other teaching options. I spent the first week interviewing at several different schools, but none of them offered me more money, or anything special. There were so many schools that needed teachers; it was just a fun adventure to see what they had to offer. Later that week I had dinner with the director of ELS International at American Pacific University. I liked her and what she had planned for the school, and accepted my original job offer.

I was to start the following week, so with a few days to kill, I decided to see other parts of Vietnam. That would include a side trip to the Mekong Delta and Vung Tau, a great place for weekends out of the bustling city, which is only about an hour away by hydrofoil. I didn't realize that a hydrofoil was unusual—it just seemed like a nice, fast boat ride to me—but I later learned that they were uncommon, built in the 1960s and a gift to Vietnam from Russia. These hydrofoils run between Saigon and Vung Tau almost every hour during the daytime, the trip usually a little over an hour. I couldn't see much in the way of sights other than the Saigon River, since the windows were sprayed with water. It was just the best way to go from Saigon to Vung Tau. There was only one other option, and that was by bus, which took several hours.

Sometimes in life, strange things just happen, and you get lucky. My first visit to Vung Tau was one of those times. As soon as I got off the hydrofoil, a young man with a taxi grabbed my pack, and said he'd take me anywhere I wanted for one U.S. dollar if he could practice his English with me. We spent a lot of time that weekend sightseeing and practicing his English. Upon my arrival, he obtained a wonderful hotel room and told everyone that I was his English teacher.

A little later at the beach, everyone there knew I was an English teacher, and within the first ten minutes people surrounded me, just to listen or look. The lady who owned the spot on the beach where I was sitting insisted on giving me free beer all day. She was also determined to watch over my pack, for security reasons.

Later, I met her entire family. One of her sons spoke English, and he invited me to dinner with his family. We all sat on the beach drinking beer in shot glasses. When someone poured a glass for you, you were to slam it back, while everyone yelled "YO!" and it was bottoms up for everyone. This was crazy fun, and certainly broke the language barrier, with much laughter, and poking fun at each other through sign language and translations.

The food seemed to be unending: one dish that I knew was a huge platter of fried quail liver, and they were fantastic. There were many different little plates of spring rolls, some rice things in banana leaves, and many strange dishes, and more beer. I call them things because I have no idea what most of them were, but they were all delicious. Each new platter had a special dipping sauce, which were tasty enough to drink all alone. My favorite was a rice wrapped goodies that I wished I knew the name of. They were spicy, but yet sweet and the texture was nice and firm, ha, ha—tasted like chicken. Oh, man was I going to love Vietnam if this life kept up! The lovely people, the food, and the beach, it was like being on a life vacation.

My trip to the Mekong Delta was a long bus ride and then a short trip by boat down the famous Mekong River. It is an awesome river, over 2700 miles and seeming to stretch forever. We visited the floating market, where everything you could ever want was sold on boats lined up together. We also stopped at a small village and had a wonderful lunch of what I believe was called Elephant Ear fish, a horrid looking thing but so delicious—and I don't even like fish that much. The little villages along the river were picture perfect, and the rural people were unique in their style of dress. Everyone in the villages rode a bike or scooter, as the roads were not built for cars or trucks. They are just small paths created during the war for foot traffic.

I had a terrible cold or allergy, so when I noticed what looked like a pharmacy or Chinese medicine shop I thought I'd see what I could get. I wasn't sure how to explain to them what I wanted, to get their attention I gave a couple of loud coughs and patted my chest. The two ladies behind the counter shook their heads and looked at me with concern. In a couple of minutes, one of them brought me a cup of something and signed for me to drink it.

I didn't know how to ask how much it cost, so I just put some dong (Vietnamese currency) on the counter. But the ladies shook their heads no and pushed my money back to me. I went to find the tour guide and explained to him that I needed his help. We went back together, and he asked them why they didn't take my money. They told him, "We have never had a foreigner want to buy anything. They all just come to look at our snakes, but she wanted to buy." And then much laughter. I gave them some dong anyway, but I have no idea how much it should have cost. Feeling much better with less coughing, I boarded the bus for a long and slow trip back to Saigon.

My first thoughts of Saigon were; how the hell do I cross the streets? The traffic was absolutely terrifying. It felt like a swarm of killer-bees, all bearing down on me. There were millions of motor-bikes, fancy new cars, old bicycles, buses, taxis, and *cyclos* (rickshaws) all using the street that I wanted to cross. It required nerves of steel to venture across the first time. Later I learned to, close my eyes for a moment, then slowly walk across a street, and hope the drivers would veer around me, but it always made my heart beat a little faster. After being in the city awhile, it became a past-time to watch newcomers attempt their first street-crossing.

The best way to get around Saigon is with a *xe om* driver (*xe* means motorbike and *om* means hug or hold). After I was there for a few days, I had my personal drivers. It is normal for the drivers to have their own area and special passengers. It seemed that all the other *xe om* drivers in the area knew not to try to steal "the special passengers" from each other.

I arranged to be picked up at 7:30 AM, Monday through Friday, and my driver was always there on the dot. I had two drivers that waited outside my hotel, and if they weren't there when I needed them, they had arranged for someone else to drive me. The new driver would always tell me, "It is okay. Your driver gave me orders to pick you up."

It took about thirty minutes to get to my school and cost about five dollars a week. It was a wild and crazy ride, as there are over eight million cycles in Saigon, and they all seemed to be on the street at 7:30 in the morning. I grew to love my ride to school; it was a good wake-up call, with the most amazing, exciting things to see every day.

My favorite driver was Mr. Long, the nicest man in the world. He had hidden from the Viet Cong during the war, as he was involved in helping the South. My other driver was Mr. Happy, who at times seemed to have smoked too many happy sticks. He would sing American songs the entire ride. Riding twice a day for many months, we became good friends. I also rode with the young boys who sat in front of the hotel or school and would beg me to let them drive me if my drivers weren't there. They were jealous of Mr. Long because it was a good job to have a daily passenger.

The other drivers all teased that Mr. Long was my husband, and I should kiss him. We all had fun with this, and even without a common language, we understood a good joke. Not many of the drivers spoke much English, so it usually meant pointing and showing the written address you wanted, but it worked. Mr. Long and I practiced his English daily, and he would ask, "What's that? What does this mean?" He wanted to be the best English-speaking *xe om* driver in Vietnam.

Most of the foreign teachers didn't hire a driver, renting scooters instead. I was the only one who didn't end up in a bad bike wreck. One of my fellow teachers and her passenger had a wreck that left one of them with a broken leg. Later my neighbor and his girlfriend had a serious accident that left him in the hospital for months and severely damaged his brain. So whenever I got the urge to drive myself, I just thought about five dollars a week and safe Mr. Long and how much I would miss seeing him. Besides, I really liked the riding and looking and not worrying where I was going.

Ho Chi Minh City (Saigon) is huge, with some eight million people, but it felt much smaller. I have never liked large cities, but I loved this one. It is alive and exciting, with each street having something a little unusual. One area may be Chinatown, with every other shop selling gold. The next street may be nothing but carpets, and the next several street might be dogs (yes, live dogs for restaurants to buy and prepare), or it could be the elegant downtown. The central city is shockingly modern, with high-rises and glamorous stores. The parks are abundant and beautiful, as are the roundabouts, with flowers by the hundreds. The city changes the flowers in the intersections, and the parks every month or when needed. The beauty of this city surprised me daily. I'd match it with any city in the world for the government's effort to beautify. At Christmas, there were more poinsettias, and Christmas trees than anywhere I had been before. After Christmas, the marigolds arrived and were everywhere. This is not just in the tourist area but in every district. It is a breathtaking city.

Going to the markets in Vietnam is a way of life. Sometimes I loved it and at times I hated it. The biggest market in Saigon, Ben Thanh, was also the one closest to my hotel. The booths were filled with vendors yelling, "Lady, lady, over here, what you want? I have everything. You come with me!" until you wanted to scream. But no matter what, at times, I had to go there.

Riding on a *xe om* really wasn't cool in a skirt. I needed pants. The only thing to do was go to the market and buy material. Shopping in the market could be an overwhelming chore, as there were aisles and aisles of fabric. Finally, I got what I thought I needed, but then I had to find a seamstress. I asked the girls at my hotel for help, and they suggested a lady just down the alley, who would make the pants for me. They would be ready the next day and cost almost nothing.

On one of my first trips to the market I wanted to eat quail, and I knew if I kept looking I'd find it. When I did find it, the woman didn't want to sell it to me. She kept bringing out different plates of shrimp, and I'd point again to the quail. I figured it was because she didn't think I knew what it was, and so she was trying to sell me what most foreigners ate. Finally, I said, "Peep, peep!" and she gave it to me with a huge smile. Then she yelled something in Vietnamese to everyone at the other booths, and laughed, and pointed at me and said, "Peep, peep!" People came and watched me eat, and then two or three well-dressed Vietnamese ladies sat down, and ordered "peep peeps." The quail was cooked perfectly, and I hoped they all loved it as I did. I think they did because they kept laughing and saying, "Peep, peeps." Who knows, maybe they are now known as the peep peeps?

One of the things I'm sorry I didn't buy was a pan to fry quail eggs. These little pans were used in both Thailand and Vietnam, just for cooking quail eggs, and those little eggs were one of my favorite street-side snacks. I've since tried to make them in a regular frying pan, and they just didn't cook as well with the whites spreading out to far, and cooking too fast. I think the special pan is the secret to good fried quail eggs.

American Pacific University was located in District 11, about thirty minutes from the central part of the city, where I lived. This district was an area where no foreigners usually were seen. So when all of us tall, blonde, light-skinned strangers showed up, we caused a daily distraction. One of our teachers was about 6 foot 5 and would get looks anywhere in the world, so you can imagine the staring he got from the tiny Vietnamese people.

Riding on the *xe om* with Mr. Long, I received many stares and actually caused a few bike wrecks. Mr. Long loved it and would point to me as he drove by the staring faces. Best of all were the looks on little kids' faces; true shock and then a big smile. I would smile and wave, and soon the kids would all wave when they saw any of us.

Our ESL teachers were an international group: American, Canadian, Korean, *Viet Kieu,* New Zealander, South African, and one from England. This was a great group of people, and we spent a lot of time together. We usually all ate with some of our students at one of the sidewalk cafés. It was wonderful and very cheap food, a meal costing about fifty cents. The only thing I couldn't eat was a pho made of blood sausage, which the male teachers seemed to like. This is a traditional Thursday pho, and I could smell it being cooked a block away. I love the regular pho, but when they add the pig blood and blood sausage, no thank you. Lunch was normally, pork chops, chicken, tofu, or unknown goodies, with rice, and a few vegetables. There were lots of food stands in our area, and they were all a little different, so it was never boring and always good food. The food was displayed under a glass enclosed case, and you just pointed to which item you wanted, or had one of the Vietnamese students order for you. There was even a Kentucky Fried Chicken on our street before I left. I wasn't sure if that was good or bad, it just showed how rapidly District 11 was changing.

Eating *pho* almost every day, I wasn't sure which I like better the *pho ga* (chicken) or the *pho bo* (beef) But I do have many recipes from my students, as this was one of our writing projects for my advanced class. My one graduating class created a cook-book, each student contributed a recipe, then the class printed the book, took pre-published orders, and sold it to people in our school. It was a real hit with my students as the profits were used for a party.

I certainly reaped the benefits too, with many true Vietnamese recipes, and Pho soup was one of them. One student's recipe reads as follows:

My Mother's Pho

First, cook some beef bones, lots of them, in lots a water, in a huge pot. My mother adds onions, some star anise, and a big piece of ginger. Cook for many hours. Let sit and get the fat off the top. Feed the bones to the dogs. Then cook your noodles in the hot broth in a special Vietnamese big spoon, Teacher you know what kind we use.

Put a big cup of Pho in a bowl, and add the noodles. Then you need those little bowls of bean sprout, basil (*la que*), lime, onions. Oh, my Mother said you have to wash the bean sprouts in boiling water, to kill bad things. Then you get to eat it and make your mouth happy. I like my Mothers best of all.

My recipe book is one I'll always cherish as a reminder of these great kids and the wonderful food of Vietnam.

One afternoon, another teacher and I were having lunch on the sidewalk near our school. As usual, the tables were low to the ground, and we were sitting on small stools, about ten inches tall. Imagine where you would be looking if a person were standing next to you. As I looked up, a young man came around the corner ... naked. Being more than a little surprised, I just kept staring at him as he walked toward our table, looking directly at me. I warned Andrea, "Don't turn around!"

But as soon as I said that, she turned her head ... right into the young man's naked privates. And when she screamed and jumped up, she spilled her bowl of soup on them. Now he was screaming and trying to wipe off the burning hot soup. Slowly, he walked over to the table of four Vietnamese ladies, and one of them handed him a napkin. Then he walked down the street, which was full of people, with not a care in the world. The ladies at the other table just kept eating. The owner of the restaurant cleaned our table and brought another bowl of soup, never mentioning the naked man.

I was still laughing, and Andrea had finally recovered and was starting to think it was pretty funny too, when one of the Vietnamese ladies tapped Andrea on the shoulder and said in English and sign language, "Rooster in face." Then all of these ladies were laughing and saying, "Rooster in face! Oh, yes, Big Rooster Face." From that day on, Andrea had a new name.

November 11 and it was another birthday for me. Having read my passport, the girls at Hotel 64 had a birthday cake and balloons for me. So sweet, and here I didn't think anyone would know. Madam Cuc had arranged it all. She gave me a couple of bottles of my favorite wine and an amazing dinner at one of the five star restaurants.

Madam Cuc, is an extremely interesting woman. This lady had somehow survived the war, and had a horrid scar to remind her, and others of what she had survived. The scar is on her throat: and her neck had been cut from ear to ear. It is shocking to see, until you see her smile, and she's always smiling. Madam Cuc is a very wealthy woman, and a powerful force in the Party. The gossip was that she had been a spy for the North. However, that was just gossip, and someday I hope to know the truth from Madam herself.

I had only been teaching at APU a week when it was Teacher's Day. Teacher's Day in Vietnam was an important day. In countries outside the U.S. teachers are very well-respected and honored. My students bought me a cute little purse, some lotion, and flowers. Then the girls from the office took me to lunch. I was quite surprised by this generous gift and became a little emotional.

Later in the afternoon, everyone gathered in the auditorium and the students all sang to us in Vietnamese. Then one of our brave teachers sang an English song. Now all the students were looking at me to be next, so I sang a Chubby Checker song and did the twist. The students were all laughing and clapping, and I thought they had approved of my performance. None of the other teachers would do anything, so I'm not sure how they felt about my song and dance routine. Oh well, they would find out that I'd do anything for my students, even the twist!

On my first payday, I was a millionaire! I made twelve million dong. Next month I would make over forty million dong. The cost of living was so low I could live like a real millionaire. With my check in hand, off to the bank I went.

That first trip to the bank was very strange. Each teacher was issued a check from APU. Then we had to go to a certain bank where APU had an account. All the teachers went to the same bank, where we were escorted upstairs to accounting by bank security, then we all sat wondering what the deal was. The accountant spoke English and she told us we had to come back in an hour. Why? No one knew. We all returned in an hour, and again we were escorted upstairs, like VIPs or criminals. We received a piece of paper, and were told to go to cashier #2, and she would give us our money. It was interesting to see twelve million dong counted out first by a money counting machine and then by the teller. All this was done, with fifty other people watching the foreigners get a massive amount of money. Like in many foreign countries the bank security stood at the doors with huge machine-guns. However, once I left the bank I was definitely on my own, with twelve million dong in my purse.

Now what would I do with it? Everyone warns you to keep your money with you and not to trust this bank or that bank. Crazy as it was, I hid my money all over my apartment. I decided the best place was under my garbage, thinking no one would ever look there, so my money usually had a strange odor. Later, I opened an account, and there was never any problem getting my money out. It just took an hour or two because of all the paper work. The bank would not trade dong to dollars, so when I was leaving Vietnam I had to go to a money exchange for dollars. Although many foreigners were paranoid about these transactions, I never had a problem with the banks or the money exchange,

My first group of five advanced students passed the Secondary Level English Proficiency (SLEP) exam. This exam is needed to study in a foreign country, and also required by Vietnam Immigration, to receive a study visa. The exam evaluated students understanding of spoken English and grammar usage. We held a small ceremony for them with speeches, diplomas, and a party.

Three of the students would go to Seattle, one to a college on the east coast and one to California. I say "my" students because I taught them half the day and Allison had them for the other half day. We both thought of them as "our" students, and neither of us had had experience with the SLEP exam, so we both felt pride and great excitement for our first students leaving APU for the United States.

APU enrolled fifty new students the first month I was at there. There was a lot of juggling of teachers as they hadn't expected this contract from Vietnam Airlines at that time. It was a little hectic, at best. The ELS department was contracted to improve these students English so that they could pass the SLEP exam and be accepted into an aviation school in Seattle, Washington. Luckily, Allison and I had succeeded with our small first group, so these fifty new students became "our" students too.

These young men, aged twenty to thirty, were from all over Vietnam. Some already spoke fair English, others not much. Some were married and would be away from their wives for two to four years. Some had never spoken to an American before coming to APU. I'm proud to say that all fifty of them, after eight months of learning, were accepted into the aviation program.

These students became like my second family. Some of them referred to me as Grandma, which is the best compliment you can receive in Vietnam. We sang karaoke, ate dog meat (yes, dog meat), and took road trips together, and I had the time of my life. One of the sweetest parts of teaching there was the friendship with our students. The teachers were treated with great respect when in class, but we could cross that boundary and just be friends out of class.

Part of Allison's and my job was to prepare our group for the transition of moving to the United States. Imagine, if you had to move to Vietnam and live and study there for two to four years. They had the same fears about the United States, only much more so. Plus one huge added stress; being Asian they felt they could not fail, or they would bring shame to their families. These students were the "cream of the crop" but still very naïve young men. Under Allison's and my protective wings, for eight months, besides preparing for the SLEP, we discussed everything we could think of about living in the United States of America, with the main focus on Seattle, Washington.

Daily, we talked and talked about it, read newspapers, Googled it; they lived and breathed Seattle. By the time I'd had them in my class for eight months, I thought they knew everything there was to know about life in Seattle. However, they needed more information about life in general, in the big world of the USA. So we talked about music and what was hot and what was not, what to wear to look like a cool dude, where to shop for Asian food, and where to eat cheap food, besides McDonald's, how to talk to American girls, and win their hearts. Well, we discussed every question anyone could come up with, and then we talked about everything, again. Allison and I did everything we could think of to keep them excited and ready for their big day.

The last week of class before they were to leave for Seattle, I asked if they had anything else they wanted to talk about. Man oh man that was a bad question to ask. They must have all discussed this earlier, and as a group said, "Yes, we want to know about sex."

I had a rule in my class, that anything they wrote would be private, and what we talked about would not leave my classroom without their permission. Vietnam is still a Communist country, and you can go to prison for saying the wrong thing to the wrong person. This was important for their protection, and I believe it was helpful in gaining their trust.

The first week in my class it was so quiet I thought I was really screwing up and doing something wrong. I asked Allison about her class, and it was the same: no one was talking. I would ask very simple questions, like: "Do you like ice-cream?" They would answer, "yes." "What is your favorite color?" No matter what the first student said, the entire class would agree. Finally, I asked one of the more talkative boys what was going on in class. He told me everything was good, they just weren't sure of the correct answers.

A traditional Vietnamese teacher walks into the classroom and starts writing on the board, the students then copy and memorize what is written. They are told never to voice their opinion, or they will be punished, and now here I was just asking for opinions. I had to assure and reassure them that there were no wrong answers and that I truly wanted to know what they thought. I promised them they would never be wrong and never be punished for voicing their opinion. And that is when I promised that nothing would ever leave my classroom.

They also were very afraid of someone in the school spying on them for the government and possibly getting kicked out of the program. I didn't know if that was a true possibility or not, but I told them this would not happen if I could help it. The adjustments they had to make to the way we were teaching and to understanding our English were monumental. They were all so very brave and admirable. I don't believe we had any students quit and return home.

Back to the Sex question. I know my face turned red, and I stammered a bit, but then I asked them, "Do you really wanted to talk to me about sex?"

In unison, they all said, "Yes, we do."

A bit puzzled I asked them, "Can't you talk to your father or an uncle or another man, maybe one of the male teachers?"

"No, we trust you, and we decided to ask you because no one will ever talk to us about it."

I threw-up my hands, rolled my eyes, wiped the sweat from my brow and said, "Okay I'll answer your questions if I can." They all had questions and some repeated questions.

These boys, my advanced class of twelve, were in their twenties to thirties, but many of them had never even kissed a girl, and the ones who were married had more questions than the ones who weren't. My only rule was that we use the proper words and no slang the first hour, because they should know the correct terms for the body parts they were asking about. I finally had to use the computer for a body diagram with correct terms, but the next hour it got down to slang and some hard facts of S-E-X.

One of the cutest questions was, what do men call breasts in the U.S.? So on my white-board I listed all the terms I could think of: boobs, knocker, jugs, chi-chi and more. This was all written on the white-board, but my room had a big window facing out to the hallway. When I finished writing I quickly erased it, a little worried what the director or another teacher might think if they walked by.

Then a student quietly asked, "What's a blow-job?" They had gotten this off some porn site and didn't understand the words. Can you imagine explaining this to a class of young men? Well, it wasn't easy, but I thought if they can ask, I can answer. It wasn't a joke to them. They wanted this information, and there was never any laughing or poking each other. It was all very serious most of the time, except for my nervous laughter. No question went unanswered, and when class of two or three hours was over every one of my students hugged me and thanked me. If there was a spy for the government in our school, I would probably be in prison now, or at least have been kicked out of the country.

One very cute thing I noticed about all the students, no matter what their age, they loved the word "love". They were always in love with someone. They loved romantic music, Valentine's day, the total love thing was true joy to them.

I always started our class with music, and if it was a love song, no matter how awful the recording was, they loved it. They sort of liked rap music, and any music that I suggested was new to the Seattle scene. Music was my way of warming them up for a relaxed conversation. We would either talk about the words to the song, how it made them feel, or new words they didn't understand. More than likely it would somehow turn into something about "love".

I loved every moment of teaching, with one exception. It was report card time again, and that was something I really hated. I wished I could just give them all passing grades and be done with it. It was an all day chore, no matter how well prepared I was with the daily grades. First it was recorded in my records, then in ELS records, and again in APU records, the secretary needed a copy, and I think even the janitor got one. In the foreign countries, I've been in, paper work is done en masse quantities, even with computers it's not simple.

We would celebrate in some way when it was completed, because we all hated the report card thing. Sometimes we went bowling, other times to a karaoke parlor or maybe for some rice wine and *ban xeo* (Vietnamese pancakes with vegetables), or we might all meet at Allison and Carrie's house to cook.

Two of our teachers were roommates and had a gorgeous home, so if there was going to be a party it was held at Carrie and Allison's house. We would all bring something to eat and drink, as they were nice enough to supply the roof-top party spot. From past parties, I had somehow become the shrimp person, and it was a fun thing to buy and fix. I would go to the Ben Tan market, where I could hand pick, huge, fresh and ever so tasty shrimp. I bought a little barbeque grill, especially for our shrimp cookouts. I loved spending the morning peeling and marinating them; with fresh spices, olive oil, garlic, and a bit of Dalat red wine.

The first time I cooked them this way, one of the Vietnamese boys was a little upset that I had ruined them by shelling them first, which is not done in Vietnam. I could tell he was really disgusted with my preparation and ruining perfectly good shrimp. But, after the first bite he started asking what I had done and how to fix them, so he could tell his mother. Joking, I told him, he had to come to my English/Cooking class.

I did take a Vietnamese cooking class with a couple of friends, and it was simply fantastic. Each of us had our own hot-plate with all the essential ingredients set up in little bowls. First we watched the chef, and then we prepared it as he instructed. One of my friends changed her recipe, using less sugar, and later we all decided the chef did a much better job than she did. What was she thinking? This man was a renowned chef in Saigon! For $35USD, we prepared a spring roll with shrimp, dipping sauces, chicken in a clay pot, a salad, rice, and a to-die-for banana dessert.

At Christmas, some of the teachers became a little depressed, many spending their first Christmas away from home. But, some good Dalat red wine and another lovely party at Carrie and Allison's helped get everyone in a better mood. Plus Saigon's lights and decorations were so festive, who wouldn't feel the spirit of Christmas.

The downtown area, from Dong Khoi to the Notre Dame Cathedral, was as well decorated as New York City, or so the girls from NY said. The parks, streets, and businesses had hundreds of poinsettias, everything glimmering with little white lights and Christmas trees of every color. Santa was not forgotten either. Saigon was truly a classy, well-dressed lady at Christmas. She was no slouch after Christmas, either, the parks and streets all quickly replanted with flowers. This was when marigolds filled the city, the flower of renewal and spring, It was quite an amazing amount of plants provided by the government.

On the day after Christmas, Indonesia and Thailand were hit by a horrific tsunami. I was so sad for my wonderful friends in Thailand and prayed they were safe. The people in Vietnam gathered food and clothing, and our school donated money. It was surprising how much aid Vietnam offered as it is such a very poor country itself. It made me proud to know these kind, generous, giving people.

TET, is the Vietnamese Lunar New Year, and what a special time they make of it. Everyone cleans and paints their homes in preparation for visitors. Flags are hung in the streets and homes, and flowers and plants are everywhere. Many people travel home during this holiday, and special food is prepared for the occasion. Children and the elderly are given little red pouches of money, to bring good luck. A week or so before the holiday everyone goes shopping for new clothes and special holiday food, as many stores close during the holidays.

The first day of the New Year is spent with just the immediate family, but the next day everyone visits homes in the neighborhood. The eating and drinking together continue for a week or two. On the first day of TET, it is important not to visit anyone's home, but one's immediate family, as the first visitor determines how lucky you and your home will be for the following year. If you are a rich and lucky person you are welcome to visit, but if not stay away!

During subsequent days, people visit relatives and friends. Traditionally, but not strictly, the second day is usually reserved for friends, while the third day is for teachers, who command respect in Vietnam. Local Buddhist temples are popular spots as people like to give donations and to get their fortunes told during this special time. Children are free to spend their new money on toys or on gambling games, which can be found in the streets. Prosperous families pay for dragon dancers to perform at their house. But, the streets are often filled with these exciting dancers, for everyone's enjoyment. This dance is said to bring good luck, and scare away bad luck.

There are many do's and don'ts during this special time, as the Vietnamese are rather superstitious. You should never say anything bad about anyone. Don't eat duck or shrimp. Don't wear white. Sweeping during this time is taboo or *xui* (unlucky), since it symbolizes sweeping the luck away. It is also taboo for anyone who experienced a recent loss of a family member to visit anyone else, as that brings bad luck to everyone in the house.. But, You should go gambling, as this is a lucky time. You should also pay all debts, and return anything you have borrowed in the previous year.

Shockingly, overnight the parks in the center of the city became filled with pots of trees and flowers. One day it was an empty area, and the next day it was covered in plants, it became more beautiful than I could imagine. There must have been kumquat trees shaped in every shape imaginable. And being a lover of orchids, I spent hours gazing at so many new and unusual ones. The orchids and kumquat trees were definitely the most popular, as these are considered to be lucky.

It's a strange time to visit Vietnam as many businesses are closed and all airlines and buses are filled. If you're in Vietnam you can't get out, and if you want in, it's impossible. Shopping for just the basics can be difficult, as the stores are either closed or their shelves are empty. It is a crazy and wonderful time. You need to prepare for TET, even if you are a foreigner.

I took a few days off after the holiday, because I hadn't prepared before hand to travel. I went to Na Trang, which is a short flight from Saigon on Vietnam Airlines (my student's airline). I loved it there, but some friends thought it was a terrible tourist town full of drugs. I will say that whenever I got on a *xe om* the first question they asked was if I wanted some smoke. That is life in many countries; either buy it or don't, it's your call. I will say after a while I wondered if I looked like a dope smoker, or if they just hoped I was.

I had a great time with the lady vendors at the beach there. I would meet them every afternoon after swimming at a pool or in the ocean. We would visit, and I would buy the most wonderful lobster or huge prawns, and everything was fresh caught that morning. We would sit on the beach, and the ladies would cook my seafood over a charcoal fire while we chatted.

One of the ladies spoke English and had a wicked sense of humor. She loved to talk about Americans, boyfriends, and bam bam (sex). She told me her husband worked nights, and she worked days, so they only had "bam bam" when she wanted to. They all wanted to know if I still had "bam bam" and who, and how many men I'd had "bam bam" with. The bam bam lady's husband was a fisherman who caught the lobster and prawns that they sold. These crazy ladies would give me whatever they hadn't sold at the end of the day, in exchange to sit and talk. Mainly, we just laughed together at their naughty jokes. I would have loved to teach there, but there was only one school, and it was new with only a few students.

After I had been at Hotel 64 for a few months, I thought I would like to get an apartment of my own. It was great fun to see these different places with my rental-agent. He told me, that all housing I would see would be legal. He explained that first the government inspected the housing, and then it had to be registered before a foreigner could live there. There were certain qualifications, like how many square feet per person, adequate bathroom facilities, and mainly the landlords standing with the police and government.

My agent would pick me up on his motor-bike and off we'd go to see his new listing. At one place, the rent started at $600USD a month, but when they heard I was an English teacher the owners said I could live there for free, if I taught their son. I met him and asked if he wanted to learn English. All he did was shake his head, negatively. Another place wanted me to live in their daughter's room while she was gone. I was to live there with all her possessions, and not change anything. One home looked gorgeous; with a swimming pool and elegant garden. However, my entry was through the back-alley, and was terrible with no lights, and a ton of garbage.

I just wanted a regular apartment by myself. I finally found one, that was sort of okay. The location was good, it was clean, and the price was right. There was only one problem. At times, I would come home and find that someone had taken a shower in my bathroom, or had just used the toilet, and it still smelled from their use. Maybe it was the boy who took care of repairs? That was normal to them. Well, not in my apartment. Then one day I came home, and someone had had sex in my bed. Yes, I know, sex. I bought a big padlock, and everything was fine from then on. I told my students about someone using my apartment when I was gone, and they just thought it was all very normal, and that it was funny that I was upset.

One night while living there, I saw two boys in the street below my apartment trying to highlight their hair. They were making a terrible mess out of it, and the boy's hair was turning green. Being an old hairdresser I had to go help. When we finished, they loved it and wanted to bring their friends. I did several Viet boys' hair blonde and made some great friends in the neighborhood. The boys' mothers weren't too happy at first, but when lots of the neighbors had blond hair they seemed to feel better.

The alleyways of District 1 were where all the foreign teachers ate, drank and met at night. This was one of the most popular areas, known as the backpacker's area, for good and cheap food. This was also where Cindy, another teacher and I were kicked out of a bar. I truly believe we may be the only foreign ladies to have ever been kicked out of a bar in Vietnam, or perhaps in all of Asia. No, we were not drunk, vulgar, or rowdy.

We had been drinking wine and visiting, when after the second glass, I noticed the waitress hadn't given me the correct change. Then when I ordered another glass, and the money wasn't right again, I told her about it and about the other time she'd made a mistake. She called the owner over and started yelling that we had called her a liar. I explained to the owner what I had seen and showed him the money that I'd paid, and the change I got back. Meanwhile, the waitress was standing in the alleyway screaming about lying American women. He told us that she was very honest and had just made a mistake.

That was okay with us, but not with her. She kept screaming, and the owner asked us to leave. We told him we would, when we finished our drinks. He pleaded with us, "Just go now and never come back, because she will scream until you leave, and every time she sees you. So maybe it's not good to come down this alley ever again." We did leave and went next door where everyone was laughing as hard as we were. Since the bars are all open to the street, everyone in the block had heard her, and knew we had been kicked out. I'm not sure that this was a good thing to be famous in Vietnam for, but it sure was funny.

During one of many holidays, a friend and I flew to Fhu Quoc Island. It was a cheap, short flight from Saigon, and we stayed at an all-inclusive hotel for next to nothing. Hot is the word for that island, hot, hotter, and hottest. We needed to get up early to go to the beach, because by noon it was too hot to step on the sand. Then we would head for the swimming pool, where they put ice in the water to cool it off.

I had a delightful experience, one morning on the beach with a local vendor that was selling little clam-like things. He understood how much I loved eating them, and showed me where to go to find these delicious morsels. I waded out along a small cliff and picked them off the rocks, and then we cooked them on his campfire. Inside their shell was a beautiful stone, and once heated the stone released from the shell, and inside was a delectable tiny clam-like morsel. I thought I had gathered enough to feed several people, but they were so tiny that the two of us ate them all by ourselves.

I also enjoyed a group on a fishing boat, lots of Vietnamese and me. It was a fantastic time because I love to fish. To have the experience of fishing with another culture was a special treat. I was curious to see if we used the same techniques or not, and what worked on the fish here. None of them spoke English, but one of the men fishing beside me, and I competed to see of who could catch the most. This was done with just smiles, laughing, sign language, and good old fishermen wit. I don't know who won, but I know the two of us laughed a lot, caught many fish, and entertained his friends with our contest. Whatever fish were caught were cooked on-board the boat, and after dark, we all fished for squid. The squid fishing wasn't very successful that night, but still a great experience.

Lesson 192---People everywhere in the world love to laugh, and some of us love to fish too.

After my nice little vacation, it was time to get back to school and prepare my students for their final days of school at APU. We had completed almost all the requirements for our advanced students' program, but my students had one more assignment to complete for me. One of my most important writing assignments for all my advanced students was to interview their grandparents, if possible, or to talk to their parents about their grandparents. I explained how important this was because this was their grandparent's history, their country's history, but most importantly it was their history. They all understood that their grandparents had lived during a harrowing time in Vietnam, and it should never be forgotten or repeated. They knew this one assignment was important to me, and much of their grade would depend on their writing.

As a teacher in a foreign country, I truly believe that the most important thing is to show respect for that country. Today everyone wants to be like the U.S. and I assured my students that their country was wonderful and as good as the U.S. and to be proud of their people and themselves. This was especially important to me, because my students were going to the U.S. and needed confidence in their own worth.

My students had their airline tickets, were packed and ready to go. Our final party was in progress, and we were all discussing our plans. I had a strange feeling that I should reconfirm my reservations. When I called the airline, I was told, that somehow my reservations had been canceled and there were no more seats available until next month. I was a little upset, and then one of my students asked me if he could see my airline ticket. He took it away and in a little while returned and told me not to worry. He had talked to his mom, and she would get me on the flight home. I just had to go to Vietnam Airlines at 7AM, and she would have a new ticket for me on Eva Air.

When I asked him, "How did you do this?"

He laughed and said, "You always told me I could do anything."

The truth finally came out when I met his mother the next morning. Both of his parents were in very high positions with two separate airlines and also well respected in Vietnam's political Party. This young man never mentioned his parents' connections, who they were, or what they did. Like all the wonderful Vietnamese, he was very humble.

I had come to Vietnam on a whim and a desire to do something to pay back this country for what the American war had done to their people and their land. However, I have to admit I had been a bit naive in my thinking. I don't know if anything could ever repay these lovely people or their beautiful country. My only hope was that I helped a group of young people to have a better life, and for these students to return from the U.S. and help other people.

Now it was time to see my American daughters, my grandson Riley and my new baby granddaughter, Lexi Genevieve. It had been difficult for me not being there for her birth, but my daughter had assured me that everything was fine and that this little girl would be waiting for me to arrive. I was so in love with my grandson, I couldn't wait to meet this new little person.

CHAPTER 13

After spending a couple of months with my American family and my Vietnamese boys, I was back on the Internet studying different countries that piqued my interest. I kept hitting Nicaragua and daily became more excited about this new idea, although I couldn't find much information about teaching there. So, one slightly rainy day in Seattle, I gave my daughters a heads-up on my plans, and with their continued approval I booked a ticket to Managua, Nicaragua.

Once again, I was leaving Seattle with a smile on my face and a ticket to Miami and then on to Managua, Nicaragua. I had three seats all to myself, so I could sleep all the way to Miami. Everything was moving along smoothly, except where was my travel guide. Then I remembered-- I must have left it in my daughter's car, along with my delicious duck sandwich. I wasn't sure, which upset me the most; the lack of my travel guide, or not having my cherished duck sandwich.

I had no idea how to get out of Managua. I just remembered that I'd planned to go from the airport to a bus station. But, which station? I knew I had read that there was more than one. Then like magic sitting cross the aisle, I spied a guy with a Central America travel guide and asked to borrow it, madly writing down locations, hostels, and the correct bus station.

While we waited for our backpacks to arrive, the man with the travel guide, and I talked about our plans. We decided to grab a cab together, as neither of us wanted to spend time in Managua. The first bus station the taxi took us to was a hellhole, and I sure wasn't getting out there. The taxi driver had made a "mistake" and made a little more money. Then he took us to the correct station at Universidad Centroamericana (UCA).

As soon as we got out of the taxi, people were grabbing at us and pushing us to get on their bus. I had been in this mess before and knew to get my back to the wall, protecting my backpack from quick hands, and just say, *"No, gracias."* Men surrounded my new friend, who seemed unaware of what was happening. We finally saw the bus to Granada, and jumped on, but my friend was minus his wallet.

Once in Granada we found a lovely hostel with a choice of dorm rooms, or a private room. I have stayed in lots of dorms and enjoyed them, but this time I could use the luxury of a private room with air conditioning. The Hostel Oasis was a great location—close to everything, free Internet, one free call to the USA, a huge collection of first-run movies, a first-class book exchange, and a swimming pool.

I spent the first few days just enjoying Granada, a picturesque city famous for its colonial architecture and museums. It is located on the edge of one of the largest lakes in the world, Lake Nicaragua, which you could walk to from the center of town. The parks in the city were wonderful, and in the evenings the locals gathered there with their families. And for the delight of tourists, there were horse drawn carriages.

The most beautiful were the funeral carriages, with the horses covered in flowers and the carriage carrying a plain or ornate casket, depending on the wealth of the deceased. During the funeral procession, friends and family walked behind the carriage, the number of followers proclaiming the sort of person the deceased had been. If he wasn't such a nice person, the family paid people to walk behind the carriage, to make a respectable show of his life.

Despite my original plan, after a few days of talking with the girls at the front desk of Hostel Oasis, I decided not to go to San Juan del Sur. They told me it was dirty, full of tourists, and everyone spoke English already. They wanted me to stay and see the schools insisting, "Granada needs more, and better English classes." They were so bossy, and persistent I told them I'd check them out. One of the girls even made an appointment for me to see the director of the American British College (ABC).

When I arrived at ABC, not only the director was waiting to see me, but the entire staff was there to welcome me. After a brief introduction, Mr. Marlon wanted to know if I could start at 4 PM that day. They were all so excited, how could I say no?

I was assigned four hours a day, and the director wanted me to go to each class and just talk to the students, because this was such a new experience for them. These students had never had a foreign teacher before and looked petrified when I walked into the class. But an hour later, I couldn't shut them up! They just wanted to talk to a real American.

I later learned that my first class (advanced level) told all the other students how cool it was and not to be afraid of the new teacher. One girl in that class was so excited to have a foreign teacher, she jumped up and kissed me on both cheeks, a big compliment in Latin America.

This class was the most advanced and spoke English quite well, but I also taught lower levels that didn't speak any English. After six months, we had to hire two other foreign teachers because the students demanded native speakers, and our enrollment had doubled. This was a huge step for Granada schools. And ABC was the first to have a foreign teacher. Proudly, that was me!

After living at the hostel for a couple of weeks, I fell into a strange living arrangement with a rich and ditzy American. This man (Mr. Rich Gringo) had sold everything he owned in San Francisco, wanting to start a new life in Nicaragua. He had somehow edged his way into ABC and was giving the owner a lot of money for improvements, so he was very popular. The only thing I saw him do was throw money at ABC and try to make his way into becoming the manager.

He had rented a lovely house close to the school and wanted me to rent a room from him. The price was right, the location great, and he had bought all new furniture—beds, a TV, the works. Although I thought he was a conniving *gringo* and had a bad feeling about him, I took him up on his offer.

Then one of the men he had befriended, a local Nicaraguan, had a problem with him. Every day they stood at the door arguing and threatening each other. I made sure that the Nicaraguan man knew I was not friends with Mr. RG and only rented from him. The Nico man told me, "He might just end up in an alley some dark night." This made me a little nervous, but their disagreement passed after a couple of weeks, and I became friends with the Nico man.

The first weekend after I moved in with Mr. Rich Gringo, when I was on my way out, he wanted to know where I was going, when I would return, and who I was going with. I explained that it was not his concern, and that I had been traveling alone for several years with no one checking on me. However, he insisted on having my daughters' telephone numbers in case of emergency. I conceded but emphasized, "The only time you are allowed to call them, is if I am dead. Do you understand?" He was such a frightened and nervous man, that I almost felt sorry for him.

Mr. Rich Gringo decided he needed to dig up the concrete courtyard, as all the other homes in Nicaragua had a garden in the center. He hired two local boys to do this horrid job of digging and removing rocks. While digging up the garden spot, they found a quart jar with a voodoo doll inside. They threw down their shovels, ran out of the garden, and told Mr. RG to burn the doll, or they wouldn't return to work. Mr. RG was a nervous wreck, and didn't want to touch it. I begged him to give it to me, and promised not to open the lid while I was in his house. He finally agreed, perhaps because he was also afraid of looking foolish to me.

Someone's wife had made this little voodoo doll when she was really pissed-off at her husband for cheating on her with her best friend. She had made the doll from his underwear and had put stick pins in various parts of his body. She had written a note telling him all the bad things she wanted to happen to him, and from the pins you could tell what parts of the body, she wanted it to happen to.

This doll is one of my most cherished items, and now sits in my daughter's house. No bad juju had ever happened to us, but I'm not sure about the husband.

Since the voodoo doll was gone, and the garden was ready to plant, Mr. RG asked if I would buy some plants for him. I found a young girl who would bring different plants to the house every day, and I could choose what I wanted. She was from the village of Masaya, called the city of flowers, and she and her mother brought plants and flowers daily to Granada. This tiny girl would carry these heavy plants on her head all day, walking the entire city. When I would help her put her basket back on her head, I could barely lift them.

I bought lots of plants from her, as the first several I got didn't have a leaf left on them the next morning. When I showed them to her, and she couldn't believe it. She gave me another one to see what would happen to it. The next morning, it was also bare. I got another plant and went to check it that night but never saw anything. Yet in the morning, the plant was bare of leaves again.

Finally, I walked into the dirt the boys were digging up for the new garden and found it infested with huge ants. They were everywhere, millions of big black and red ants. I hadn't seen them before because they didn't travel during the day unless disturbed. When I disturbed them, they took huge bites out of any greenery in their path before scurrying back into the dirt. The next day my little plant girl brought some chemicals to get rid of these nasty buggers, and from then on, our plants were healthy and happy.

Mr. RG had found a couple of other people to rent his rooms. Happily, Laurel, a new teacher at ABC, had rented one of the rooms. We were both smokers and it drove Mr. RG wild, although he knew about it when he rented to us. But he wanted to keep the owner of ABC happy, so he had to let us stay. In the evenings after work, Laurel and I played cards, drank a few beers, laughed, and smoked.

One night Mr. RG came out to the kitchen where Laurel and I were playing cards and told us, in his drunken voice, "You have to move. After months of not sleeping from your laughing all night, your smoking making me sick, and your drinking all that beer starting me drinking again, you need to find another place to live." Then he went to the kitchen sink and threw up.

We had been evicted! We both thought this was absolutely hilarious. Neither of us had ever had the honor of eviction. We had to come to Nicaragua for this experience.

By that time, we both thought Mr. RG was a little unbalanced and were ready to leave anyway. But I would miss our nice little house, perfect except for him. Shortly after our eviction, he opened his own English school and tried to ruin ABC's reputation. Predictably, his school never got off the ground.

Lesson 80: Always go with your gut feelings and good instincts.

Granada was a quiet small town and very safe if one exercised a little judgment about where to go, especially at night. It was one of the most popular tourist towns in Nicaragua and the most picturesque. It was also becoming quite modern, and drugs had found their way to some of the local kids. The favorite seemed to be "whiffing" glue, the cheapest high in Nicaragua. These young street kids had the most vacant look in their eyes, the damage to their brains irreparable, and were now begging on the streets. The government kept talking about mandating that glue be kept in locked cabinets, but it hadn't happened.

There were many restaurants in Granada with great food and high prices, but the average food in Nicaragua wasn't the best in Latin America. If it wasn't deep-fried, they didn't cook it. I did find a café—open only in the morning and afternoon— that offered nice fresh food.

There was always an old lady sitting on the steps when I went there for lunch. I noticed that the local people always gave her their leftovers. She didn't look as poor, or as hungry as some beggars, but there was something special about her, so I gave her mine also. One day I asked the waiter about the old lady. He told me, "She gives this food to the poor and the hungry." So from then on, I ordered an extra meal, especially for her. She would give me a huge toothless smile and shake my hand, saying a dozen times, "*Gracias, amiga, gracias.*"

During Semana Santa (Easter week) each country south of the USA holds a special celebration unique to their country. Nicaragua seemed to celebrate for at least a month. I lived across from one of the biggest churches, and it was the custom to light huge firecrackers, more like small bombs, on the stairs to the church, daily at dawn. The kids carried this religious tradition a step further, lighting these nasty bombs day and night. I never got used to it and wondered how a country that had seen so much bloodshed could tolerate the sound of gunfire. I tried to leave Granada as often as I could during this noisy time.

Laguna de Apoyo was my favorite weekend spot. It's a huge lake in an inactive volcano about six miles from Granada, and The Monkey Hut was where I hung my hat. It was a sweet little hostel that had cooking facilities, beer, wine, kayaks, a great patio for lounging or sleeping, clear cool water to swim in, and howler monkeys right next to the sunbathing deck. Instead of roosters waking you in the morning, it would be the sound of several howler monkeys. I usually rented a dorm room, but then I'd take my sleeping pad and move to the porch to spend the night, listening to birds and watching the stars.

The manager was a Rastafarian from the UK, and we became great friends. He told me that he wasn't treated very well in Nicaragua because of his long dreadlocks. The Nico men made fun of him, calling him *señora*, and the Nico women never looked his way except to laugh. I know it is said that Rastafarian men treat women poorly, but this man always treated me with kindness and respect.

I met some strange and wonderful people at The Hut, but one of my favorite stories is about two men from Belize. We had spent the day swimming and playing cards … and then out came the tequila. One of the men was a rich *gringo*, and the other was a friend/guide/translator from Belize. The more tequila we drank, the more loving the Belizean man became. He asked me where I slept, and I explained that I usually slept on the deck, but tonight it was going to rain so I would be sleeping inside. He said, "Well, no little rain is going to stop me. If you want to join me later, please do so."

I pulled my sleeping pad out, and the lights went out as usual around 11 PM. Soon I heard someone walking by my bedroll to the deck, then back to the beer cooler, and back to the patio. Then I began hearing a lot of sexy noise, but at that point I covered my head and went to sleep.

The next morning I asked my Belize friend, "Who was the woman with you on the deck last night?"

"Jesus Christ, I couldn't believe you were really coming out to see me. And then you were pouring cold beer in my mouth, when you weren't kissing me all over my body. I thought you were going to give me a heart attack."

"Okay, but you know it wasn't me, who was it?"

"I don't have any idea. Are you sure it wasn't you?"

Laughing, I told him, "You know damned well that wasn't me."

We checked the room I thought I'd heard her come from, but there was no one there, and my Rasta man swore no one had rented the room that night. The local people said that strange things happened at the Laguna, and we both agreed. Perhaps there was a ghost among us that night.

Getting to the Laguna de Apoyo was easy if you took the truck from the Bearded Monkey in Granada. But this never worked for me, as their bus only ran Monday, Wednesday, and Friday and I had to go on Saturdays because of teaching. So I'd take the Masaya bus, get off at the entrance to the Laguna, and then hitchhike to the Monkey Hut. The first time I hitchhiked, I was a bit nervous, but if I didn't want to walk four or five kilometers, this was my only option. Supposedly, a bus ran to the bottom of the hill, but no one knew when.

When my daughter Brandi came to visit, a trip to Laguna de Apoyo was the first thing we did. I hadn't said how we were going to get there, so when we got off the bus from Masaya, crossed the highway, and I sat my pack down, she asked, "What now?" When I told her we would just stand there until we caught a ride, she started laughing and said, "Oh, God, Mom, who else but you would think of hitching a ride."

We were picked up within a few minutes by three young men in a van. They were from the U.S. and said they would take us down the hill but not to the bottom, as their church wasn't that far down. They were Jehovah's Witnesses, and I had to laugh because these religious men were the only people I ever hitched a ride with who didn't take me all the way to the Monkey Hut.

We spent a few days enjoying the water, playing games with other guests, hiking, boating, and being happy. Bran met a young man to show her the rest of the island. And I got to enjoy some time with my Rasta man.

Catching a ride out of the Laguna is easy. You stand at the gate of the Monkey Hut and when a pickup truck comes by, you just jump in the back and tell them, "*Vamos a* Granada." So we were in the back of a truck, each of us with a cold beer in hand for the road, when halfway up the mountain, the truck stopped, and two men slowly climbed in with us. One of the men was huge, maybe 300 pounds. We thought he might die, he was breathing so hard from the steep climb up the side of the volcano, so I offered him my beer. He drank it all in one gulp, and wanted to know if we had more.

When we got to Granada the driver wanted to take us directly to my house, not just drop us off downtown. On the way, we made a stop so the big man could buy us a six-pack for "saving his life." I accepted it and gave one to everyone in the truck. He told me thanks, but good manners would have been to just accept his gift and drink it all ourselves. This was not the first manners mistake I'd made in foreign countries.

Later that night Brandi and I went to one of my favorite fancy restaurants, Viejo Gringo. The food was always good, and their guitar player, Three-Finger Jimmy, knew any song you asked for. Whether he would play it depended on who asked. He never played what I wanted. But he fell in love with my daughter, so if I wanted a certain song, she'd make the request. Three-Finger Jimmy was also the owner of the restaurant, so we had a great dinner, with him doting on all our (Brandi's) whims.

That particular night, one of my adult students had invited us there to listen to him play his guitar, but instead Jimmy wanted to show off his own talent for Brandi. My student sat with us most of the night instead of playing his guitar, and ended up getting a little *borracho* (drunk). In his drunkenness, he was asking me to move in with him. I laughed and this really got his Latino pride riled up. He said even his mama would be happy. She would do my laundry, cook for me, and be so very proud to have me living with her son. Listening to all this silliness, Brandi was wide eyed and giggling. She loves it when young men ignore her and hit on her old mom. At that point, I thought it was getting a little whacko even for me. Then he got on his knees and started begging me, "You can have your own room. Just please move into my home."

I told Brandi, "*Vamos*, now!" and we left quickly out the side door and ran home, laughing over the *loco* Latinos.

I wanted my daughter to see all the good places I had found in Nicaragua, so we caught a "chicken bus" to Rivas. From Rivas the best way to get to San Juan del Sur was to catch a taxi, $5 USD for as many people as you could fit in. We shared our ride with a middle-aged Nico lady. Just to be polite and make conversation, I complimented her on the lovely ring she wore. She took it off and gave it to me! This ring was no cheap thing; it may have been her wedding ring. She was disappointed when I refused it, repeating, "Please, please, you take," and pushing it into my hand. But I just couldn't take it; all I had to give her was Mexican silver jewelry, which is so common no one in Nicaragua would want it.

Lesson 180: Do not tell any woman in a foreign country you like something she owns, because it will be yours.

San Juan del Sur was a popular vacation spot for Nicos and their families. It had a great beach and was the place to see turtles laying their eggs. Around the bay from San Juan was a popular surfing area, and many rich foreigners had homes on the hillside, overlooking the city and the bay.

It was the Christmas holiday, and we had no reservations. After looking all over town, we found a room way up on the hillside in an old and formerly fancy resort. I was sure it was closed and someone had decided to rent rooms just for the holidays. Nonetheless, we sunned our buns, danced in the street with everyone, gambled with the Nicos, and had a lot of fun.

At night the streets were so packed, it was hard to move. Some of the beach bars had put up fences around their businesses because the year before it had gotten so rowdy that two of the bars were completely ruined. The bars looked like jails, and I wondered how you would get out if it did get too wild. Needless to say, we didn't go in. Our nightly treat was fresh prawns for dinner and then dancing in the streets with the wild and free local people on holiday and celebrating Christmas.

On one of my visits to San Juan del Sur, I took a trip with a local guide and four other foreigners to a protected national park to see the *tortugas* (turtles) laying their eggs. We packed a picnic, climbed into the back of an old jeep, and traveled for about an hour on almost nonexistent roads. It was a beautiful secluded bay, and we spent the late afternoon swimming, hiking the beach, and watching the local monkeys. Just before it got dark, the park ranger met us and told us to come quickly, as he had found a turtle nest hatching.

The ranger carefully moved a layer of sand away from the eggs. Immediately, the egg on top started to crack open. All the eggs below seemed to start vibrating. When the top egg was fully cracked, out scrambled a baby turtle. He was digging into the sand, slipping back into the hole, and then trying again. One by one, the eggs below cracked open and the entire nest was alive with movement, one baby after another scrambling in their race for survival. As we watched them all scurrying toward the water, I thought how tiny they were to be cast into that vast ocean. It seemed an impossible journey for these little creatures.

Shortly after this amazing birth, the ranger told us he had spotted turtles in the bay, but it could be a while before they decided to come ashore, so we should sit quietly and be patient. When it was pitch black, we saw a big shadow moving toward us. We all held our breath, hoping it would keep coming our way. Soon she lumbered over to us, and we had to move slowly out of her way. The ranger had told us that when the pregnant turtles came ashore, nothing could stop them from going to their birthplace. The females return to the exact spot on the beach where they were born.

We had two ladies only a few feet apart, busily throwing sand every which way. They knew how big and how deep their hole needed to be before they started to lay their eggs. It was incredible how much sand those little fins could dig and how far they could throw it.

After about forty-five minutes our lady started to settle in, and we could hear her moaning and see her pushing. At one point, I was only a few inches from her face and saw the eyes and soul of this wonderful animal. I had witnessed many animal births, but this was an unforgettable experience. I would always remember those eyes.

Our guide carefully dug some sand away so we could see the eggs as they were being laid. We were allowed to take pictures at this point, because nothing was going to stop her from her job. When she finished, she started pushing sand back into the hole, and once again we were told to sit very quietly so as not to disturb her. We quietly left, and as we walked back along the beach, we counted twenty mamas laying their eggs.

Watching those turtles, I thought about a sad story my friend Ernesto had told me. He was a young boy working on a commercial fishing boat out of Mexico. They had been at sea a long time and didn't have much food left, when the captain saw a huge *tortuga*. The captain ordered Ernesto to jump into the water, giving him his knife and telling him to kill the turtle. A young and gentle boy, Ernesto told the captain he didn't want to do this. The captain answered, "If you don't do this, I'll throw you in and leave you to die."

Ernesto swam over to the *tortuga* and held her in his arms, swimming with this beautiful sea animal. Then he stabbed the knife into her. He said, "She looked into my eyes, and then she cried tears, real tears, and her eyes were just like those of my mother's." At that moment, he didn't care if the captain left him to die or not, because he felt like he had just killed the most beautiful thing on earth. He never went on another fishing boat.

Telling Brandi about these experiences, we wished it was *tortuga* time. Instead we had to leave this fun spot and get ready for our next trip. Since I had a two-week vacation from classes, I had booked tickets for us to Big Corn Island. I hadn't been there yet, but it sounded like a place we needed to see. Strangely, when we told people we were going, everyone said the same thing: "No, don't go there. It's a terrible place. You will be robbed, raped, and murdered." Nevertheless, we already had tickets, and it looked interesting in the travel guide, especially for the fishing.

We had to go back to Managua and catch a plane from there to Big Corn Island. Managua was never fun, a big, dirty, scary city, but we survived and caught our flight to Bluefield, and then on to Big Corn Island. We arrived with a plane full of Nicos and one other foreigner. The foreigner didn't have reservations either, so we joined up and hired a taxi to take us all to the beach.

Finding a hotel wasn't a problem in fact, we may have been the only tourists on the island. Our hotel wasn't anything to get excited about, but it was right on the beach. Then the rains came. It rained and rained and rained. The only things to do were kill mosquitoes, drink rum, play cards, and laugh. We would take a taxi to other parts of the island, have another rum, and eat whatever they had, as there weren't that many options. Nicaraguan food isn't great, but I thought Big Corn Island, being on the Caribbean, would at least have some good lobster or shrimp. Wherever we stopped, my first question was "Do you have lobster today?" No, was the answer at every restaurant on the island.

With the entire time spent in the rain, we didn't learn much about Corn Island, other than it had good rum, lots of mosquitoes, and the people weren't as happy as they could have been. It took several days before the bartender at our hotel would even look up when we asked for another round, and that is just not normal, anywhere.

We couldn't get to Little Corn because of the high seas, which was a disappointment to me. We weren't robbed, raped, or murdered, in fact, one of the above might have added some excitement.

After Brandi left for the States, I still had a few months to travel around Nicaragua on the weekends and holidays. One of the most famous sites in Nicaragua is Ometepe Island, which sits between two active volcanoes. My teacher friend Laurel and I caught the bus to Rivas and then to San Jorge, where we took the ferry to Ometepe Island. The ferry ride was about an hour long, and the boat was packed with local island people and four or five foreigners. Again, it was a spur of the moment trip, so we had no reservations, but we were sure it wouldn't be a problem.

The only problem was the ferocious rain and lightning. Very few of the roads were paved, so the taxis wouldn't go anywhere off the main highway. This meant a trek on foot through the mud, in the dark, with only one flashlight. We finally did find a hostel, which didn't have a room or beer, but they said a hostel just down the beach had rooms and maybe beer.

After more mud, more rain, and much more lightning, dodging rocks, trees, and the tide coming in, we finally found the hostel, and thankfully, they did have a room and a beer. There was no electricity because lightening had hit something, so it was pitch black. Everyone was sitting out by the campfire, which made for quick friendship and a good party. When I saw Laurel's mud-covered face in the glow of the campfire, I realized what I must look like, but no one seemed to mind.

The next day the rain continued, and we were stuck in the hostel most of the morning. But by afternoon it had cleared a little, and we could see where we had been walking the night before. We had trekked through a farmer's field where a huge bull was now standing guard. I was glad he hadn't seen us the night before. We caught a ride into town, but the rain started again, so we quickly caught a ride back to the hostel. We didn't see much of the island but a campfire, a bull, a lot of rain, and the volcanoes lit up at night by the lightning. But, all and all it was a fun time. When it rains for days and your traveling companion still isn't getting bitchy, it must be considered a good trip.

I was once again leaving people and a country I had grown to love. I adore traveling by bus to see the countryside, so I decided to take a bus from Granada, Nicaragua, to Antigua, Guatemala. From Granada to San Salvador was an eleven-hour trip through mountains, hilly farm land, and down to the ocean before arriving in San Salvador, where we would overnight at the San Carlos Hotel, owned by the Tica bus company.

The San Carlos was a clean, little hostel but not in the most desirable part of town. The bus driver and hotel staff warned everyone not to venture out, as there had been too many robberies of bus passengers in that area. When I crossed the street to a little restaurant, the waiter looked at me as if he had never seen a *gringa* before. After I had finished eating, he insisted on walking me back to the hostel, although it was just across the street. Needless to say, I didn't get to see much of the city.

The next morning we departed at 6 AM, after the hotel had given us coffee, rolls, and lovely scrambled eggs. It was only four hours to Guatemala City, so I took a little catnap after seeing the sun rise above some volcano or another. I had seen this part of Guatemala before, so it was okay to take a quick *siesta*.

Arriving and departing Guatemala City as quickly as possible, I caught another bus to Antigua. I had been told that *Semana Santa* (Easter week) in Antigua was one of the most unusual and beautiful times to be there. My first stop was to see if Ruth, the owner of my original home stay, had a room for me. She told me my old room was available and joked that she needed to go to the market to buy mayonnaise for me, saying that Lionel would be thrilled to join me later for a ham sandwich. After getting settled, I went to say hi to the teachers at the Spanish school I had attended in the past.

The next morning I was up early, as Ruth had explained that no one slept late during Holy Week, or they would miss the beginning of one parade or another. It being Palm Sunday, today's parade would be the most solemn and one of the largest. I could hear drums and clanging cymbals approaching our street. As the music got louder, the crowd became quieter. Then I saw hundreds of men and boys in purple robes, the smell and smoke of incense overwhelming.

Slowly around the corner came the *andas* (float) with an image of the Holy Virgin of Sorrow and Jesus of Nazareth, supported on the shoulders of the purple-robed *curcuruchas (*carriers*)* This float weighed about seven thousand pounds, and it took sixty to a hundred *curcuruchas* to carry it a block, after which other men joined the march and took over. The parade lasted about twelve hours, covering most streets and finally arriving at the main cathedral.

The *alfombras* (street carpets) were the reason I had come back to Antigua. Every house or business on the street made their own sawdust carpet, and Ruth's was no exception. Our group started the *alfombra* at 5 AM, since we had to complete it before noon. We first covered the cobblestone street with sand and then laid down a cardboard pattern. We had flour sacks full of different brightly colored sawdust, which we sifted over the pattern. This took four or five hours, the pattern being quite intricate and the "carpet" perhaps twelve by twenty feet. After we gently lifted away the pattern, the edges were decorated with fresh fruit and vegetables cut in delicate shapes. We finished just before noon and sat enjoying our backbreaking work.

Then I heard a lot of noise and looked up to see several people on horseback galloping down our street. In a heartbeat, our *alfombra* was destroyed. I was shocked, to say the least. Ruth laughed and explained this was why we had to be finished by noon, the time the horsemen were scheduled to arrive on our street. When I asked her why everyone made these masterpieces only to have them ruined almost as soon as they were completed, she answered, "Simply to show the hard life of Jesus and show your willingness to follow his life."

While I was thankful to have experienced a part of this beauty, I was ready to head back home to my family. I usually tried to arrive back in the States in the warmth of June or July, but even though I knew I'd freeze, it was time to return. So I caught the little bus back to Guatemala City and once again flew back to Seattle.

I may like to think I'm some foot-loose, fancy-free woman but the reality is; I'm a mom and a grandmother, and those ties never loosen. Returning "home" to my family is always the best adventure anyone could ask for, and then leaving once again is bitter sweet. I'm a fortunate person that even my grandchildren understand that Grandma Choo Choo will be going to some other country, soon.

I love the name my grandson gave me when he was a baby, Grandma Choo Choo. He learned early that I was a traveler, and he related me to the coming and going of the train. He always picked me up at the train station and left me off there when we had to say good-bye. So smartly, I was his grandma that went somewhere on the train. Later he knew what country I was in, and would tell his pre-school teachers all about the country, and what I was doing there. He still thinks I can speak every language in the world. Well why would I tell him any different? I love him thinking I'm so brilliant.

CHAPTER 14

After spending a month with my family, I decided I needed to see South America. I loved what I'd seen in Central America and now wanted to go farther south. I had studied up on Venezuela, and I thought that would probably be my final destination, but I also wanted to go to Colombia. After a debate with myself, I booked a ticket to Bogotá, Colombia, with plans for Cartagena, being the most important, and then somewhere beyond.

A serious fisherman will tell to you never give away your favorite fishing spot; otherwise, when you come back it will be gone. All your friends, their friends and their friends will be there and your secret will be out, and the fishing will suck.

That is how I feel about Colombia. It's like a nice little secret. Most travelers hit the "Gringo Trail" from Mexico to Central America and then maybe on to Ecuador and farther south, but few of them land in Colombia.

Once again, as I started to talk about my next best place to see, some people asked, "Do you think Colombia is safe?" I had no idea how safe it was as I was sure I had read the same things they had read, but it didn't sound that dangerous to me. I had a Nicaraguan friend who told me I must go there, as Cartagena was the most beautiful city in the world. She had traveled there alone, and didn't understand why people avoided Colombia. So with her encouragement, I decided I must go see what she thought was so special.

The flight from Seattle to Bogotá landed late at night, and to my dismay, no taxis were outside the front door. However, there was a lovely lady who asked in perfect English if she could help me. I told her I needed a taxi and a hotel for the night. She said not to worry, that was her job, grabbed my backpack, and told me to follow her. After we crossed the street and a taxi pulled up, she set my pack down and started to lecture me on Bogotá, what to do and what not to do, all in a very stern voice and shaking her finger at me. She told me she would take me to a nice, inexpensive hotel close by and return for me in the morning.

True to her word, she took me to a sweet little hotel, bartered for a better price, and made sure my room was okay with me. My original plan had been to spend a few days in Bogotá and then take a bus to Cartagena, but she convinced me this was not a good idea, as the bus was extremely dangerous at night and the trip took twenty hours. The next morning she picked me up, and we were off to the airport to get the ticket for Cartagena, that she had arranged for me. When she dropped me at the ticket counter and hugged me goodbye, I tried to give her a tip, but she declined and told me it was her job to make sure all foreign travelers were safe and happy. She was paid by the airport and the government of Colombia.

As the plane approached Cartagena, I could see the beautiful blue-green, crystal clear ocean, dotted with large and small boats. This was the city, I had come to Colombia to see, and from the sky it was as lovely as my friend had said it would be.

As I waited for my backpack to arrive, I listened to a new tone of the Spanish language, much more rapid than in Mexico and also totally different from that of Nicaragua. Later I understood it to be the sound of the Caribbean, and it began to sound like Spanish music to my ears.

I didn't have reservations, but reviews of the Hotel El Viajero sounded promising. Although the airport was only a short distance from the "old town" area where it was located, it was slow going with dense traffic on the narrow one-way streets. The taxi driver told me it was normal during rush hour for nothing to move but a few feet at a time. As we approached my hotel, he told me I needed to pay him and then jump out as we passed the yellow building. The street was so narrow and crowded, he couldn't pull over.

Luckily, Hotel El Viajero had a room available which I grabbed and quickly departed. I was anxious to see this most beautiful city in the world. The cobblestone streets were charming, and the homes with their bougainvilleas and geraniums hanging on wrought-iron balconies were the sweetest I had ever seen. Cartagena is known for the great walls protecting the city, giving it a different charm than the usual beachfront town. The fortress, built to protect Cartagena from pirates, made me feel as if I'd gone back in time. I could almost see Captain Hook climbing the walls.

My favorite spot was El Centro, or the San Diego area, where there was always something exciting to see, and lots of interesting places to eat and drink. At night, there were performers of some sort until the wee hours. The Caribbean dancers, their entire bodies vibrating, shaking, and gyrating to the wild drumming music were incredible. I didn't know a body could move that way, and that drums could sound so sexual. These dancers performed here nightly. There were also fire-eater, clowns, and young kids doing break-dancing or acrobatics. It was a crazy place to enjoy life.

Being a tourist destination, Cartagena had restaurants of every cuisine and price, but I normally stuck to the street food and ate with the local people. The *butifarras* (meatballs) and *arepas de huevos* (fried dough with an egg inside) were my daily sidewalk meals, along with a cold Aguila beer.

Not only is Cartagena a beautiful city, but a very romantic city, with horse-drawn carriages, roving musicians, and old-time gas lanterns to light the streets, it also is home to some strange museums, like the Palacio de la Inquisicion. Upon entering, there was a figure clothed in black with an executioner's hood, followed by a chamber with a rack and other torture tools. The courtyard held a gallows and chopping block, both used to execute witches. From the looks of all the different ways to execute, there must have been a lot of witches. Although I found it a bit too weird, it was the number one tourist attraction.

Plaza de Bolivar was more tranquil and had the usual fountains and churches, along with a huge statue of Simon Bolivar. When I wanted good music or food or drink, this was where I went. This plaza was also where the shops for rubies, emeralds, and gold were located. Outside each shop, beautiful young men and women invited you inside. I hoped they didn't figure out that the reason I went into their shops wasn't a craving for jewelry but for the glorious air-conditioning. It was hot—over 100 degrees almost every day.

Cartagena was an easy city to hang out in and do nothing, but I was seriously looking for a teaching job. After two weeks of seeing the sights, I spent my days with the receptionist at my hotel, using the telephone to arrange interviews. In the evening, I gave the receptionist's son English lessons, and he gave me Spanish lessons and tips on where to go and what to do at night. He was only fifteen years old but somehow knew all the best places to dance or listen to music.

Whenever I heard a local person speaking English, I would ask where they had learned it. It was usually only two or three different schools, so those were the first I contacted. At each school, it was the same reply: "Oh, wonderful! Do you have a work permit?"

"No, but I'd like to get one."

They invariably answered, "If you will sign a one-year contract, we will help you obtain one, but you must leave the country, get a work permit while in another country, and then return."

I thought the work permit was a little pricey, considering you would only get paid five to six dollars an hour. I knew I could teach in all the big cities without a permit, but that wasn't where I wanted to live. I made the decision to keep traveling, and when I read more about Santa Marta, it sounded like what I was looking for.

One of the hardest things about traveling is leaving new friends. After having spent a couple of weeks entertaining the housekeepers, receptionist, and her son with my funny Spanish, we were all friends. On my last night in Cartagena, we went to a Cuban bar and restaurant to celebrate. My fifteen-year-old friend drank and danced us all under the table, so I understood how he knew about all the hot spots. Apparently, you could drink and dance at any age there, if your parents allowed it.

Very early the next morning, bleary-eyed and tired, I crept out of my hotel for the bus station and left for Santa Marta.

Wow! Was my first thought upon seeing Santa Marta, and after living there for two months, it became my true secret love. In Santa Marta, everything was easy. The beach, with white sand and almost a mile long, was right in front of your face, and the *Malecón* (oceanfront walkway) was captivating, day and night. The crystal clear water was a lot cooler than I expected, but it was so hot every day that the cold water was a treat.

It amazed me that Santa Marta was only ninety-five miles from Cartagena, yet there were no foreign tourists. I was the only blonde on the entire beach for months, except for the occasional Colombian woman with bleached hair, and I stuck out like a sore thumb. After the first few days, the kids, all knew my name. When they saw me, they all yelled, "Hello, Donna!" then lowered their heads and giggled. I met a boy about twenty years old who spoke English, and he gathered a group of kids who truly wanted to learn English but had no money. Every afternoon, we practiced their English or my Spanish and swam together when we got too hot.

It was the best feeling in the world to be in Colombia, South America, and to be so welcomed. When I walked down the *Malecon* people thanked me, and vendors gave me free treats. Even the crazy lady with dreadlocks to her knees blessed me. I had been kissed by more strangers there than by friends in the United States. And all this was just for spending time with a group of poor kids and teaching them a few words in English and how to laugh and be comfortable with a *gringa*.

I fell in love with Santa Marta and wanted to stay, so off I went looking for an ESL school. I knew the people here needed English, as very few locals spoke even a word. The first day I was lucky enough to find the Centro Colombo Americano, a school that wasn't concerned about a work permit and was excited to have an American English teacher. As in many countries, it wasn't unusual to pay someone to overlook legalities. The director knew many of the people in local politics and had students who were government officials, so the work permit wasn't a problem. The legal papers "were in the mail."

My students were mainly teenagers, which I loved. They were so happy to practice their English with an American that we would meet at the beach on the weekends for extra practice. They would even walk or drive me home from school because they wanted me to stay safe. They all thought I lived in a bad, bad neighborhood, full of prostitutes and drugs, and many of them offered to let me live in their homes.

I didn't think my neighborhood was so bad. The prostitutes were all friendly and wanted to learn some English words, usually naughty ones, but they were cute about it. And I never saw any indication of drugs, although I'm sure they were there. The people at my hotel and the locals in the neighborhood were very protective, and I rarely went anywhere when someone didn't ask where I was going.

The Colombian teachers were all extremely pleasant to me and always wanted to know if everything was okay, or if I needed anything. Even the school accountant would ask me if I was getting enough money and sometimes overpaid me, saying, "Jimmy said it's correct." Jimmy, the director of our school, didn't want the Colombian teachers to feel they were paid less than an American. However, I didn't think they would care because they were so happy that the students and everyone there could hear American English and learn it correctly, or so they said.

Taganga, my other secret love, was only fifteen minutes and less than fifty cents away. It was a quaint, little hippy town, with lovely beaches and much warmer water than Santa Marta. It had a few more foreigners on the beach, but still not many. It also had the best English book exchange in the area, and I needed books for complete happiness. My students from school and I went there almost every weekend, because the locals also loved this little spot.

The people in Taganga weren't as friendly as in Santa Marta, perhaps because they had more foreigners, mostly from Europe, and they didn't seem to like them very much. I was lucky to have my group of kids with me, and the people there becoming friendlier bit by bit. But still there was a difference in their attitude. Until very recently it had been a small fishing village and then quickly had become a small tourist spot. I imagined the fishermen just wanted to fish and not be bothered with transporting strangers to another beach, although they made more money that way.

One weekend my Spanish teacher, Juan, his girlfriend, Vicky, and I went camping. I didn't know where we were going, but they said it was better than Parque Taroyna, which was supposed to be fantastic. Juan assured me that all I needed to bring was a swimsuit, blanket, and beer. They would have everything else. Not knowing how primitive our camp might be I brought a couple of chickens, in case we caught no fish, and all we had were beans.

To my surprise, these kids definitely knew how to camp. They told me they did this every month and now had everything they needed for a nice trip. They even had sleeping cots (no sleeping on the ground). We had fantastic food: shrimp, clams, and fish we caught with a net. We were somewhere near Parque Taroyna, but in a perfect bay with no other people, and a mile long beach with blue-green, sparkling water. This was the classiest camp I've ever seen, and I've done a lot of camping. These kids could make a million dollars taking tourists on this same trip. Even if I knew where it was, I'd never tell, in hope of it remaining for years to come.

Not to sugar-coat Columbia, it wasn't perfect and without its share of nasty people, bad food, and other less than ideal things. My hotel wasn't the Grand Palace, the bed was awful, and both the electricity and water were intermittent. But everything was clean, and the hotel people were always delightful.

The food in Santa Marta was basic, nothing like in Cartagena, unless you went to a resort. I ate a lot of chicken, beans, and rice. My favorite chicken place was connected to a bar where the bartender had tried to cheat me out of a few pesos on my first visit. When I complained that the change wasn't correct, and the bartender totally ignored me and walked away, the man from the chicken restaurant came to help me, setting things straight with just a couple of words. We became friends, and he and his girlfriend also became my paid private students.

One night I was at their street stand talking with my friend, "Chicken Man," when I noticed a drunken woman walking toward me, looking at me with an evil eye. When she got up close, we both realized she had bad up her sleeve and was going to spit on me. He quickly pushed her back and told her to get the hell out of there. She stumbled away, cussing at me. That was the end of the problem in my eyes; however, my friend and the people on the street who had seen it were terribly embarrassed by her actions. One lady told me, "The people in Colombia aren't bad like that woman. Please excuse her and don't think badly of us."

Damn those visas, they always need to be renewed before I'm ready to leave a country. In most countries, you could simply go to immigration and get an extension, but not in Colombia. Even the people at my school couldn't pay anyone off for this much needed document. That meant going to Panama or Venezuela for a border run. I decided on Panama, but I hoped to return to Santa Marta and Taganga before too many people discovered my little secret. Strangely, I had planned to go to Venezuela before I spent time in Colombia, but my friends from Colombia despised Venezuela so much I just couldn't go there, or at least not now.

Again I needed to tell friends I cared about good-bye. I think the most difficult, were those darling kids from the beach. They had changed from shy, nervous kids into confident little people, excited to learn, play, and were now able to be carefree with a foreigner. I was so proud of them and terribly sad to leave them. I would even miss the crazy Rasta lady with dreadlocks to her knees, who followed me home from the beach every day, chanting strange songs. I would miss so many people here, but I would also miss this wonderful country.

As I sat on the flight from Santa Marta to Bogotá, I thought about the questions I'd been asked before I went to Colombia: "Is Colombia safe?" I never had a big problem there. It is the only country I've visited where I wasn't approached to buy drugs, and friends said it was very difficult to get weed even. I had found the country of Colombia to be a lovely place to live and teach, with people opening their homes and hearts to most foreigners.

It was time to board my flight from Bogotá and on to Panama City. I didn't get to see if my little Colombian Angel was at the airport in Bogotá or not, but I hoped she was still there helping lost travelers.

Arriving in Panama City I wasn't as excited as I should be. Instead of the usual thrill about experiencing a new country, I was feeling a little depressed, doubting Panama could be half as sweet as Santa Marta. But there I was, so I checked the well-worn pages torn from my travel book for an area that sounded interesting to me. I chose the old city of Panama (Casco Viejo), as I normally prefer the older areas to the modern parts.

My usual routine in a new country was to exit the airport as quickly as possible, light a cigarette, and watch for other people with big backpacks. Then I had to forget shyness and ask where they were going, hoping they were heading to the same area I was, and that they were open to sharing a taxi with an older traveler. So there I sat on top of my pack, trying to spot a friendly backpacker.

I noticed two Latino or Italian-looking guys with huge packs and quickly approached them with my best smile. It must have been my lucky day; they were from Colombia. We chatted for a bit and then the three of us shared the cost of a taxi. When we asked the taxi driver about decent hostels, he recommended a couple of places. But when we got into the old area of the city, I saw the cutest Volkswagen van painted in wild colors—a true old-time hippy van—parked in front of a hostel, and thought that had to be the ideal spot. The best part was that the owner of the van, and manager of the hostel was from Seattle, and he willingly became our chauffeur, and drove us anywhere we wanted.

My friends from Colombia were homosexuals. When I asked them what being gay was like in that country, they laughed and said, "Totally crazy." Although Colombia was supposed to be the most accepting of gay people in all the South American countries, at least politically, they said the discrimination problems at their university were horrid, and that their parents were worried about their gay lifestyle. Their lives had been full of hatred expressed toward them, which was why they had come to Panama, where they didn't have to hide their gayness from anyone. To me, they were just two very nice men, gay or not, and I felt lucky to have such fun and interesting traveling companions.

We all wanted to see the Panama Canal, one of the wonders of the world, but after looking it over and watching the huge ships pass through on their way from the Pacific to the Atlantic, we got bored and decided to take the train to Colón. The train followed the canal most of the way, so we could say we'd seen the Panama Canal from top to bottom. The train was elegant but cold—our saving grace the free hot coffee. It was about an hour trip one way, but certainly long enough for us. We had been warned by the conductor not to leave the station, as the area around the depot was a horrid, crime-ridden location, so we just had a brief stop and re-boarded our train back to the city.

Back in Casco Viejo I spent the next day or two exploring the old town and a little of the new, thanks to a mistaken bus trip. The old town was charming, with elegant churches, encrusted in gold, cute new shops, and the presidential palace. There weren't many restaurants in the area, so I needed to go farther from my hotel than I wanted at night. Luckily, my Colombian friends felt the same, so we ventured out into the dark streets together, a little surprised to see military police on almost every corner. Returning to our hotel after dinner, it was comforting to see the police again, but I made a decision to get out of Panama City and find a more relaxed spot on some beach.

I chose Bocas del Toro, a postcard-picturesque town on the Caribbean. It was so small you could walk the entire city, and that became my daily exercise. The only negative thing about Boca was it wasn't easy to get to any decent swimming beaches. Everyone took a boat to the next island, three or four minutes away, for a good beach. Luckily, one of the men at the hostel rented a boat to use for his job every day, so I got a free trip back and forth. Ken had an incredible job; doing nothing but watching over an island a rich American had bought and was planning to develop. After we checked that no one else was using this man's private paradise, our boat captain would take us out into the Caribbean to explore undeveloped islands, beautiful beaches, or we'd bring out the poles and do a little fishing.

I was staying at a lovely little hostel called Heike's by the Sea. Heike's had only five rooms and was the cleanest, best place on the island. Almost everyone there was staying for several months and worked somewhere in Boca. So it was everyone's home, and I was just lucky to have fallen into it. There was also one room for overnight guests, so we were never bored, and usually entertained by travelers coming and going.

One of the women who dropped in for a night or two had been on a volunteer project to save the *tortugas* (turtles). The project was on an island about thirty minutes from Bocas, but a million miles from comfortable living. She had paid over a thousand dollars to sleep in a tent, provide her own food, and be awakened twice a night to patrol the beaches from egg robbers. This poor woman was so mosquito-bitten it was tragic. We all told her not to return, but she had paid and was determined to complete her "adventure." What had sounded like a great escape from England had turned into a miserable month for this poor lady. Heike felt so sorry for her, that she didn't even charge her for her room and planned to report the project to the local officials.

Heike was from East Germany and had married a Panamanian man. They had opened a hostel in Boca many years ago, sold it, and then built this new one, which was not yet finished. Heike was well skilled with a hammer and saw, and since I had similar building practice, she allowed me to help with the last room. She had many talents other than carpentry. She was also a fantastic painter and singer. As a child, she had been chosen by the East German government to become a gymnast, and was required to leave home at age six and go to a camp to be trained for the Olympics. Heike spent her entire youth at this camp, only returning home for short vacations. She spent years trying to forgive her mother and the government for what she called "her prison sentence". When she turned eighteen, she crossed the border into West Germany and never returned. She met Louis there and married him to escape Germany.

I loved Louis, the most laidback person I'd ever met. As long as Heike was happy, Louis was happy. She was the builder, and he was the cook and housekeeper. We would all pitch in for groceries, Louis was head chef, and we were the cleanup crew. Sometimes a few local friends of theirs would join us for dinner, which usually became a real fiesta with Louis's gourmet meal, dark rum mojitos, Heike singing, and laughter until dawn.

After playing, playing, and much more playing, it was time for me to go back to see my family. So I made reservations to fly out of San José, Costa Rica, much closer than returning to Panama City.

I caught a speed boat at the pier in Boca, and we quickly headed out into the Caribbean, which was familiar because of previous trips with my friend, but then we moved into a river. Our boat began to slowly work its way deeper into what I would call a natural canal. It became narrower and narrower, with vines hanging over head creating an exquisite canopy. The smell was like being in a flower garden with hundreds of different flowers in bloom all at one time. There were monkeys, birds, trees, and flowers by the hundreds that I had never seen before. The silence was amazing, when the driver cut the engine and used a pole to push the boat along. It was like what I imagine the Amazon might be in places, so enchantingly beautiful. After about an hour we arrived at a little portage where buses were waiting to take everyone to the Panama/Costa Rica border known as Sixaola.

I have crossed a few borders, but this was one of those to laugh about for years. I was glad my backpack had lightened up a bit, because we had to walk across a railroad trestle with huge holes, over old rotten timbers, and an open view of the Sixaola river a hundred feet below. It was at least a hundred degrees with no shade, and a darnn long walk. This is the border crossing everyone laughs about and writes blogs on, and it certainly is sketchy despite being between two popular tourist countries. Of course, I made it safe, sound, and giggling all the way, but it just seemed strange for it to remain in such bad condition for so many years. Maybe that's the beauty of crossing here; just to say you did the Sixaola Crossing. With our passports stamped, we were loaded onto a bus for our journey to San José.

Sad but true, I didn't do anything in Costa Rica, as I was there for only two days, and it rained and rained the whole time. What a delightful day I spent in my bed with the rain beating down while I read The Boy in the Striped Pajamas. With nothing left to read I caught my flight to Seattle, where I wouldn't have time to do anything but play with my grandchildren.

CHAPTER 15

Sitting on the plane to Seattle with no book to read, I daydreamed about all the incredible places I had been and some of the near disasters I'd encountered.

In 2003, I applied for a job in China, and received an offer of employment. My school was to be located in Foshan, in Guangdong Province in the south of China, near Hong Kong. Within a week of signing the contract, SARS became the big news in the U.S. The television and newspapers were full of pictures of people wearing face masks and reports of school, business, and government closures.

When I e-mailed the school, they responded that they knew nothing of any health problems in China. I was waiting for my airline ticket to arrive from my school in China, so I sent another e-mail. Two weeks later, I received a reply that all schools in China were closed until further notice and that my ticket had been canceled.

I had a teaching friend from Wales, who took a job there. He left London on a Friday, arrived in China, and was taken to his appointed school somewhere in the boondocks, dropped off at the little one-room school and was left in front of his school, alone. He did not speak one word of Mandarin, and no one in the village spoke a word of English. His rent-free house was in a small corner of the school; it had a bathroom but no running water. He hailed down a passing taxi and returned to London on the first flight out. He was back at the local pub the following weekend. Everyone wanted to know when he was leaving for China. His reply, "Hell I've already been there and back, and don't intend to go again." That was enough for him, and this man was a world teacher and traveler. I felt lucky after listening to his story, that my school had been cancelled.

In 2004, a huge tsunami hit Phuket, and broke my heart. I was so worried about my wonderful friends at the hotel and on my street. I have since returned, and this street seems to have survived without destruction, although the street has changed a lot. Sadly, I never found any of my friends from the neighborhood. Now, I wish I had said, "Pad Thai loves all of you, and yes, Pad Thai loves Mimi."

In 2005, I applied for a job in Khartoum, Sudan, and was not only accepted but also offered more money than the original amount, because I was a woman. This should have been a red flag, but I thought it sounded like a great adventure. Thankfully, my daughter Ginny asked me not to go, as she felt it was too dangerous. Sudan is a Muslim country, with no smoking or drinking, and women must cover their bodies from wandering eyes—not exactly my kind of place. What was I to do without smoking, an occasional beer, and covered from head to toe, in the hot weather.

Immediately, after turning down the Sudan job, I applied for a position in Yemen listed on the Internet. After a couple of weeks of e-mailing back and forth, there was only one more step before finalizing a contract: a telephone interview. The lady I interviewed with was lovely, and we chatted for quite a long time about education, Muslim countries, my experiences, and when I could arrive.

Then she said, "Oh, I have another question I have to ask. How do you handle problems in the classroom?"

I told her, "I don't recall ever having a problem with students, but maybe that is due to my age."

"How old are you?"

"I'm sixty years old," I answered, although I thought it strange she didn't know this from my application and resume.

"I'm sorry, but the country of Yemen doesn't allow anyone over fifty years old to enter on a work permit. And to work in Yemen, you must have this permit."

I stopped applying to that area of the world, as age is a factor in all the countries of the Middle East. Slowly, I had slowly learned that in all the Middle East, a woman had to cover her body, no smoking, and certainly no drinking in public. I would have probably been stoned the first week, and I mean with rocks, not marijuana.

In 2007, my daughter and I were vacationing in Thailand, and I told her about this lovely island that we needed to visit because of its beauty. Well, in 07 Phi Phi Island was a sad place and showed little signs of recovery from the devastating tsunami. The glorious bay I had walked out into and saw fish swimming at my feet, was now a strange, shallow, muddy mess. The beach was no longer edged by elegant hotels, it was nothing but construction madness.

During that vacation, we spent a month on a little island not far from Koh Phi Phi. While there we met Phat, a man who had been on Phi Phi when the tsunami hit.

Phat's story was so scary that I wondered if I ever wanted to stay anywhere on a beach again. He told us of spending his life in Phi Phi, and knowing the ocean well, since it was his livelihood as a diver. On the day of the tsunami, he saw the entire bay empty, and he instinctively knew to run. He didn't know it was a tsunami, but whatever it was he knew something was terribly wrong, and he needed to get to higher ground. His biggest concern was that his brother was also on the island, and he didn't know where he was. He ran to the Phi Phi Hotel, which was the highest building in town, and then thought that it wouldn't be tall enough, so he took off for the mountain. He said, there were people running everywhere. A lady in front of him fell and couldn't make it, so he grabbed her and carried her to the hills. When he looked back at the bay, the water was black. A huge wall of water came in, and the bay emptied out, then another enormous wave came in, and the bay was empty again, until he couldn't look any longer. He watched boats, hotels, and trees being thrown like little toys—and the huge, huge, waves took his beloved village away. He stayed on the hillside for two days afraid to come back because almost everything in the town was gone or was floating out in the bay. The only positive thing he had to say was that both, he and his brother survived; but poor Phi Phi and many other places were destroyed.

In 2007, I also applied for a job in Sri Lanka. In the past, I had applied for and not been awarded jobs teaching hotel staff at a resort in the Maldives. I still dreamed of going there, supposedly home to the most beautiful water in the world. When I saw a job opening in Sri Lanka, I thought it was so close to the Maldives I could zip over there on the weekends. The director of the Sri Lanka program and I e-mailed for a couple of weeks, and I was ready to go. Then he dropped a small bomb on my head, and informed me that my school was in the center of the country in a tiny village, "safe" but, on the edge of the Tamil civil war. I quickly realized this wasn't for me, especially if it wasn't on the beach, to say nothing of not wanting to be a part of their war.

See, I'm not completely crazy! However, I will admit I'm addicted to new experiences. I love the newness of a country and its culture, getting lost and finding my way back, figuring out bus schedules, and all that goes along with the unknown. Sure, it can be scary at times, but it can also make you feel like you have conquered the world by just finding your hotel. Ok, so there was no Sri Lanka or Maldives for me now, but perhaps someday.

Not to be stopped, I was back on the Internet looking for a new destination. I wanted to go somewhere other than return to Mexico or Vietnam, so why not Thailand? I had vacationed there a few times, but never taught school there. I applied for a job in a small city close to Bangkok and the beach. Quickly, I received a contract, bought my ticket, and headed off, contract in hand.

As the school had promised, they met me at the airport and delivered me to my new home in Petchaburi. I was surprised to meet my two male roommates, one from Australia, the other from Canada. They had neglected to mention that I was to share housing, plus my free beach home housing that was promised, was only available during the weekdays, when I should be teaching. The most important thing they had not told me was that my job had been filled. They thought I should have arrived sooner and had hired someone who had just walked into their office, so I couldn't start teaching until after the month-long holiday. When you sign a contract in a foreign county, it is about as valuable as toilet paper and can be used for the same thing.

This was an annoyance to me, but there were two young people from Canada in the same situation. Except these kids had no money, and this was their first ESL teaching job. While I may have been upset and told the school what I thought about their hiring scam, I had other options. I e-mailed my old school in Vietnam, APU, and the director told me there was a job waiting for me.

However, the two kids from Canada had no idea what they were going to do without money or a job for another month. The school in Petchaburi gave them free housing for the month, but they still had to eat. My heart went out to them, along with a small loan.

A few months later, I started receiving payments from these kids, and reports of how terrible it was at their school. They were in classrooms with thirty or more very young children, and entertaining them was their sole purpose, with no attention to their learning English.

Once again, the universe had taken good care of this wandering woman, and another near disaster was avoided.

CHAPTER 16

Maybe I was always looking for something new and exciting, but it felt fantastic to be back in Vietnam. It was comforting to know an excellent job was waiting, and reservations already made at my home away from home, Hotel 64.

As I exited the new international terminal in Saigon, I heard a voice call out, "Donna!" Outside, hordes of people were waiting to pick up passengers, as visitors were no longer allowed in the terminal. Looking around, I saw one of the secretaries from American Pacific University (APU) waving at me. It was a surprise to both of us to meet at the airport, but she was even more surprised when I told her I would see her tomorrow at school. With a hug, she welcomed me back to Vietnam and APU.

Instead of getting an adrenalin rush of the unknown, I sat back relaxing. I felt like a well educated world traveler, knowing how to grab a taxi and how much to pay, instead of wondering where I might end up. I just told the taxi driver to take me to Hotel 64, on Bui Vien. My driver, Phong, spoke excellent English, and we chatted about where I was from and what I was doing in Vietnam.

Then he began the usual game of hustling customers for another hotel, telling me that Hotel 64 was not a pleasant place to stay and terribly expensive. He insisted he could find me a much better place. I understood that if he took me to the other hotel he would receive a commission, which could easily provide food for his family for a week. Nonetheless, I told him I was sorry, but I had to stay at Hotel 64 because everyone there was a long-time friend of mine.

As Phong opened my door, the girls from Hotel 64 rushed out to greet me. It felt as if they were my long lost daughters. Then Madam Cuc, possibly the most entertaining and colorful woman in Vietnam, arrived with hugs, and laughter, not to mention champagne.

Shortly thereafter, my longtime *xe om* driver, and dear friend Mr. Long appeared. We did our body language talk, with smiles and hugs, and then I jumped on the back of his motorbike for a trip to my old school in District 11. It was lovely to see the familiar faces of several of the young women working in the lobby. I was greeted with hugs and *ciao ba* or *ciao co*. Both mean hello, but *ba* is for older women, and *co* is for female teachers, to show respect. I addressed the girls with *ciao em* because they were younger than me.

After a short visit and a bit of gossip, I made my way to the office of Miss Binh, the wealthy owner of the school. A serious, unsmiling woman who could be a little scary at times, she had never been one of my favorite people at APU, but the English department had its own administrator, so I didn't have much personal contact with her. However, one day she informed me that I smiled too much and should be sterner with my students, recommending that I observe the Vietnamese teachers and learn how they presented themselves. This became an inside joke with the ELS staff, whenever we had to deal with her.

When I finished my meeting with her, I hurried out to see everyone upstairs in the English department. It was like I had never been gone. There stood Teana, the director of the ESL program, along with fellow teachers Thomas and Drew, and suddenly several high school students I knew burst into the room. There were many new faces too, and I could tell they were wondering what all the commotion was about.

After that heartwarming welcome, Teana and I slipped away to her office, where she asked what classes and levels I wanted. Once again, I would have a class preparing students to take the SLEP exam, which she knew was my favorite, and I also had the advanced conversation class—a dream comes true for an ESL teacher.

I had approximately twenty young men and five young women from Vietnam Airlines in each class. Once again, I fell in love with my students and quickly fell back into my old lifestyle of teaching and enjoying the street life of Saigon.

Bui Vien is one of the main streets in the backpackers' area, and there was never a dull moment. I loved to sit in front of my hotel, watching the unending parade of locals selling everything from fruit, CDs, massages, and marijuana to sex and dried squid. Then there were the book ladies, cashew boys, and kids selling cigarettes. Next came the ladies with trays full of nail clippers, fans, tissues, giant vibrators, everything and anything you'd never want. After the second or third day, the vendors didn't bother trying to sell me anything; they would just smile or sit with me to rest.

I did have my favorite book lady. She was much older than the usual sexy girls who carted their books for twelve hours a day, trying to sell old English novels to tourists. It was a cutthroat business, with dozens of girls selling the same books on the same streets. This older lady would arrive on a motorcycle around eight at night and hit each restaurant on the street. If she sold a book, she would sit and chat, if not she quickly moved on to the next stop. I loved her for her smile and politeness, and I often gave her my books to resell. The vendors only received a small commission on their sales, but I hoped she got to keep the money from the books I gave her.

On my second night back, I ran into my favorite street kids, Muey and Diem, and they were as excited to see me as I was to see them. Diem and I had become friends one night when two drunk foreign men were trying to teach her how to give people "the finger." Diem, was a little girl of eight years old who sold gum and cigarettes on the streets. I was extremely angry with these men, and told Diem, "Come with me!" Then I bought her a soda at the restaurant next door and explained that those men were being very, very bad, and she should never do that to anyone because it was dirty, nasty, American stuff, and to stay away from them.

The next day Diem told Muey that I was the lady, who had protected her. Her mother had told her that I was her protector on the street, and she should go find me if she was in trouble or scared. Sadly, her mother wasn't always there to protect her, since the street kids would work one area while their mothers were working at another. Frequently, when I was at a restaurant, Muey and Diem would show up, and I'd ask if they were hungry or wanted a cold soda. Sometimes they were hungry, but often they would just sit while I ate, talking and laughing with me.

These kids were delightful little people, not beggars but young street workers with families and friends. They spoke fantastic street English, and were great little salespeople. This would be their life forever, selling one thing or another on the streets of Saigon. They always had a smile, and they always made me smile.

The other wonderful thing on the streets of Saigon was the *pho*. I loved it, and every *pho* shop was "same, same but different" (a popular Vietnamese/English saying on t-shirts and other souvenirs). I ate *pho* at least twice a week and usually at a different location, and they were "same, same but different" each time. *Pho* is a noodle soup with raw or cooked meat—beef, chicken, tripe, or meatballs—with onions, herbs, bean sprouts, chili, and limes on the side, possibly the healthiest, most incredible food in all of Asia.

I loved to watch the street barbers, with their little shops on the sidewalk, giving shaves with a straight-edge razor. It always tickled me to see the barber chair, with mirrors, sitting out on the sidewalk, with customers lined up waiting for their shave or haircut.

The strangest sight was the men on the street who cleaned people's ears, using the scariest-looking, long, pointed, spiral tool. I never had that done, as it just seemed too dangerous. I did have the lady with the hot cups give me a treatment. She heated the glass cups with a small torch, then placed them where I said I had a pain. When it was finished, I had big bruises (giant hickies) where the cups had been. Was the pain gone? Well, I didn't actually have any to begin with; I just wanted to see what it felt like. I also had acupuncture done a couple of times, to see if I could quit smoking. It was a fun experience, but didn't work for me.

Weekly, I had massages at a famous massage school for the blind. I enjoyed the massages, but most of all I admired these students and their knowledge. One of the students told me my correct age just from the feel of my body. I have to say I was not happy about that, as I had hoped she would think I was much younger.

This school was a wonderful opportunity given to the blind people throughout Vietnam, by the government. Everyone thought it was one of the most helpful training programs that the political party had started. It is now a self supporting center, and highly respected by locals and tourists alike. There are so many disabled people in Vietnam, due to agent orange. It is heartbreaking. Sadly, there are not more of these types of programs to help the victims.

Of course, many things had changed in the time I had been gone, but some things never change. They just get bigger. I found that to be the case when I went to the market. I had to check my favorite spots. The snakes in their little cages always attracted a crowd, and I found it fascinating to see the vendor chopping up these living things to be eaten somehow. The snake blood is a coveted item, but I never did taste it (that I know of) although I tried snake soup once and found it delicious, yes, like chicken soup. I also had to see what strange, fresh fish they had. As a fisherwoman, I found them all intriguing and hoped to catch some of these odd creatures one day.

In need of groceries, I went to the supermarket (much smaller than any in the USA) for my favorite treats. Dalat red wine, my favorite of any in the entire world, was number one on my list of necessities. While I had been gone, they started producing many varieties, but after an hour of searching, I finally found my favorite. I would have to carry those four bottles up four flights of stairs to my room, but it was worth it. I then went in search of my Laughing Cow blue cheese. Vietnam is the only place I have found this, and I could eat my weight of it. Then I just needed to find the tiny, tiny dill pickles, the best I had ever eaten. At last, I was ready to settle onto my bed, with all my much loved treats, I'd gathered at the market.

Mr. Long, my driver, loved to take me on my weekly trips to the supermarket, along the way stopping at the little Vietnamese shops to buy lotus flowers. After that, it was on to another shop for some duck and maybe two different stops for my dill pickles, blue cheese, and wine. Then I would buy him lunch if he had time. He liked that I spent my money with the small shop keepers and not the big

Americanized stores, and he always made sure I got a good price on everything.

While back in Vietnam, I decided I should buy some new glasses. I had my prescription with me, and there were eyeglass shops and optometrists on almost every block in the central area. I asked Mr. Long where I should go, and he delivered me to a district far from the tourist area. The people there did not know a word of English, but Mr. Long took care of everything. All I had to do was pick out the frames.

We returned two days later, and when I put on my new glasses, everything blurred and I couldn't see a thing. I mimed to Mr. Long and got out my prescription again, shaking my head and looking as sad as I could. Two days later we returned, and they were perfect, with everyone smiling and nodding and shaking my hand. I was glad I hadn't bought them downtown where everything was super commercial.

Returning with my new glasses, across the outskirts of the city on the back of Mr. Long's motorbike, with the breeze in my hair, and the smells and sights of Saigon, I wondered why I had left and how I would ever again leave this wonderful country.

Yet, once again, my students had passed their much needed SLEP exam and were leaving for Seattle, so I was going along to help guide them into a new life in America. These students succeeded beyond any expectations. They all completed a two or four year degree in aviation, and returned to work for Vietnam Airlines. One of these students is back in Seattle, working on a Masters Degree in Aviation. Thanks to the Internet we have kept in touch through-out the years, and I have been able to witness; their graduations, marriages, and even a baby or two.

I had been back and forth to Vietnam so many times, a friend asked if I had weekend passes on the airline, or a Vietnamese lover. After a few months, I returned to Vietnam to teach again, but not at APU. American Pacific University's, ELS department had been disbanded while I was gone and was now only a high school.

My new teaching job was at Vietnam US Society (VUS), a huge ESL school with four or five campuses throughout the city. It was a novel experience to teach in such a large school (our campus had over 500 students), but the pay was great and my class size was usually only about twenty students. And the nicest award I ever received was from this school.

All the teachers from each campus were invited to a formal Christmas party. No matter what the occasion in Vietnam, there are many speeches by many people. Since it was a party and we were celebrating, several of us went downstairs to the bar to wait for the speeches to come to an end. When I returned upstairs, the director of my school was upset because I had received the Best New Teacher award from our campus while I was in the bar. Although they gave out dozens of silly awards, this one was important to me because the students voted on it, not the administration.

I did get to read the students' remarks about why they had chosen me. One student wrote, "When I first saw our new teacher, Ms. Donna, I was disappointed. She was an old woman with strange jewelry. First of all, I don't like old people and think they are boring, plus she had strange jewelry on her arms, neck, and even her ears. But after the first hour with Ms. Donna, I knew I was wrong. Her class was different from the other teachers, and she made our boring book interesting and fun. The best thing about Ms. Donna is that she doesn't keep looking at the clock like our other teachers. When the buzzer goes off at the end of our time, she always says, "Oh, no!" and means it. I know she likes us and likes teaching us, and that is why we all voted for Ms. Donna. I still wonder why she wears that strange jewelry, but now I love it and her."

I also taught special classes called "Talk Time" which were usually about ninety percent women, quite unusual in Vietnam and different from APU. They were mostly business women, more modern and better educated than the conventional woman in Vietnam. We had a designed program to follow, but I had the autonomy to do whatever worked for the students. This was a conversation class, and I was free to discuss anything and everything with them, except political problems in Vietnam.

However, my discussion on sex didn't go over well. Those modern young women informed me that people in Vietnam don't talk about that sort of thing. And when I kept pushing the subject, the entire class looked down and wouldn't raise their heads until I gave up on the subject. When I again asked a few questions months later, like whether their mothers had taught them about menstruation and whether they ever talked to their girlfriends about having babies, one of them said, "Teacher, remember we don't want to talk about that."

One of the lovely things about teaching in Vietnam was the long holidays. During one of the breaks, I met my daughter Brandi in Bangkok, and we flew to Phuket for some sun and fun. I don't know what was going on there, but all the hotels were full. We did finally find a room but only for one night. The next night we were able to find another room and, after a few drinks and dinner, called it a night.

Somewhat later in the night, Brandi woke me and whispered, "Mom, something is biting me. I itch all over."

Being a sleepy mother, I just said, "Bran, just cover up your head and go to sleep. It's only mosquitoes."

After a short time, she shook me again and said, "It's really bad!"

I turned on the light. "Oh, my God! Oh, my God! Can you breathe?"

Her face was twice the normal size, blood red, and her eyes were swollen almost shut. I was afraid she might not be able to breathe because her throat, arms, and legs were also swollen. She assured me that her breathing was okay, but the itching was awful.

I told her, "We need to get some ice and try to find a doctor."

As we ran downstairs, I was yelling for someone to get a doctor. But there was not a soul in the hotel, and we had been locked in, with a huge chain around the outside door. Finally, we crawled through a little window into the kitchen and found some ice. Since Brandi was still able to breathe, we went back to our room.

I told her, "Don't turn on the lights. Get our flashlight." We were horrified to find that bedbugs covered our bed! While they hadn't bothered me, poor Brandi was obviously allergic. We sat in chairs all night, waiting for someone to arrive at the hotel.

When the manager finally arrived, I was spitting mad. I tried to control my mother-hood temper, but you should never make a mother worry about her child, or you will have the wrath of God down on you.

When I told him of the bed-bugs, he became furious with me and said, "You must have brought them, because we never have bugs in our hotel and the real problem is not bed bugs, your daughter just drank too much gin, and she was probably having a gin disease."

Well let me tell you I rearranged his thinking about that very quickly.

Then when I told him about being locked in the hotel, his reply was, "It is for the protection of the hotel, if you do not like our rules, you should leave."

"Oh, yes, we are leaving, and you do have bed-bugs, you little ##%&^."

We found another nice hotel within a few minutes, where Bran spent two or three days, with cold-cloths on her face, neck, legs, arms, and various other bitten places. I explained that my daughter wasn't really ugly, in fact, in a couple of days she would be beautiful, but with the hugely swollen face, I'm sure they didn't believe me or care. When she finally looked decent enough to travel, we quickly left Phuket and flew to Krabi, where we caught a boat to Koh ??? my secret island.

Koh ??? Secret Island was like heaven. No! I won't give away the name, because it is just to perfect to share. We had a little bungalow on the beach. I went squid fishing every night with one of the local fishermen and caught buckets of them. Bran had a lovely Muslim man, who showed her the island, and fell in love with her. We spent the mornings' gathering sea-shells for a young girl to make jewelry. Then daily we had Thai massages. Life was good! We were both happy! The people on this island were totally awesome. They are Muslim, but I believe if all Muslims were like them, this world would live in peace and love. They were such friendly, happy, loving people. We had planned to spend a few days there, but we ended up spending the remainder of our vacation.

It was Christmas time, and we were invited to exchange gifts and enjoy a seafood dinner with the Muslim people from the island. Unsure what to buy for gifts, we asked Phat, Brandi's new boyfriend, to help us with our shopping, and he took us to a grocery/gift shop, where we bought some food, booze, and jewelry. It was just like any Christmas party with friends, lots of joking about gifts, laughing, and a little drinking and dancing, but we felt privileged to participate, being the only foreigners invited. Later that evening hundreds of kite lanterns were lit and set adrift into the night, a shockingly beautiful sight from the lovely Thailand beach.

During another holiday, I traveled to Cambodia, planning to stay in Phnom Penh for a few days before going on to Sihanoukville. When I arrived in Phnom Penh, I grabbed a little *tuk tuk* (similar to a big golf cart), and the driver took me to several hotels, but they were all horribly dirty and smelly. In front of every hotel and restaurant, there were enormous piles of garbage with dogs digging through it. Finally, I found one that didn't smell or have piles of garbage outside.

The next morning I found a brochure advertising a tropical garden tour. It sounded like a pleasant and fresh-smelling day, but when I walked into the garden, the first thing I saw was a wall of human skulls. Cambodia is full of sites with the remnants of the Khmer Rouge, and I did not want to see any of it. I quickly left the garden, and decided then and there to head straight for the beach of Sihanoukville.

Sihanoukville, was a little beach-front tourist area, but I didn't care I just wanted a non-smelly place to enjoy a short vacation, and perhaps meet a few Cambodian people. The beach was charming not overly clean, but okay. The food was delicious, much like Vietnam's. The people I met were used to tourists, and some were overly friendly (for the money), and others just didn't seem particularly happy. This certainly wasn't the true picture of Cambodia, but just an area to relax.

Traveling on the bus, mostly what I saw were rather sad tin shacks with many skinny, hungry-looking people, and lots of little bedraggled kids hanging around. I found the trip somewhat depressing and was anxious to return to Vietnam.

Again I had spent about nine or so months in Vietnam and loved every moment, from my students, the markets, the food, my rides back and forth to school, the city, and my home at Hotel 64.

I'm making plans now to return in the fall of 2011 and I can't wait.

SUMMARY

I haven't been around the world but, "I have seen more things than I remember, and remember much more than I saw"--- so said Benjamin Disraeli, and I feel the same.

I remember the smells of every country. On almost every street in Saigon, there was a pho restaurant or vendor. *Pho* is a fabulous, rich broth of beef or chicken, and noodles with its little bowls of bean-sprouts, basil, lime, and chili peppers. It is so similar to the *pozole* in Mexico that at times, I forgot where I was. Mexico's *pozole* is the same rich broth, but with hominy instead of noodles, with condiments of avocado, cilantro, lime, and chili peppers. Both *pho* and *pozole* are said to cure hangovers, or kill a cold, and taste better than chicken soup.

Thailand's street food could drive me to eat hourly, with the aroma of *pad thai, tom kha gai*, to my delicious chicken gizzards on the barbecue. Even the platters of bugs and larva began to tickle my appetite. Perhaps the grasshoppers, beetles, and various worms weren't for the squeamish, but after a taste or two, they were like eating popcorn or chips.

Of course, Mexico's taco stands with the fragrance of cooking meat, frying onions, and fresh cilantro caused me to gain many extra pounds. Guacamole may not have a distinct odor, but if I could smell tacos, I knew there was a big bowl of wonderful, beautiful guacamole waiting to pile on my tortilla.

Along with the good also comes the bad, and both Thailand and Vietnam have their share of horrid, stinking food. The scent of squid vendors with their torches softening their dried squid was never appealing to my nose. The fish sauce from Phu Quac was twice as smelly, but added to any Asian cooking improved the flavor, so it is always in my kitchen. Then there is the nastiest smell in all of Asia, the "king of fruit," *durian*. It was such a horrifically, pungent stench. I could smell it a city block away. *Durian* has been described as having a succulent, creamy filling, but smelling like dirty gym socks. It is much worse than any dirty gym sock, but more like a huge whiff of sewer gas. This horrid fruit, is loved by most Asians, but few foreigners can get past the rotten odor to try it.

The sounds of each country remain with me like a familiar and well loved song. The mornings in Saigon were like nowhere in the world. The young and old people of Saigon were early risers. At 5AM, the city started with a slight rumble. By 6AM, it was roaring with vendors setting up their wares, sidewalk cafes preparing for the breakfast rush, pots banging, and morning greetings yelled to friends. The parks, were filled with young and old, men and women doing exercises or martial arts. By 7AM, the roosters have finished crowing, and students and workers were beginning their day. The local markets were busy with women buying food, visiting with friends, or eating *pho* for breakfast.

In Mexico and farther south, in the beach towns, everyone seemed to come alive when the fishermen returned from night fishing. The women came to buy their fresh fish, and enjoy the daily gossip. The men went off to work, or started their serious game of chess, and the kids came outside to play. Even the rooster waited for the fishermen's return to start their crowing. The joy of each boat returning home safely, could be heard and seen with lots of high-fives, laughter, and hugs, every morning.

Thailand's morning sound could be entirely different from Bangkok's twenty-four-hour noise to the quiet of the islands and villages. At 6AM, in Bangkok the street parties might be ending, while vendors and markets were setting up for the day. However, in the quiet south, the only noise might be the morning chants from the mosques, or the gentle sound of the waves hitting the beach. I found them both equally charming and lovely sounds.

The most unforgettable of all are the people I was honored to meet. I thank each of you for the lessons you taught me. I may have come to your country to teach you English, but the life lessons you taught me are beyond belief. You showed me the beauty of your country on several back-country road trips. You even took me fishing, camping and to your favorite night spots for dancing. You allowed me to participate in traditional ceremonies of weddings, baby showers, and sadly funerals. Most of all you taught me to love every culture in this world, for how it is. Your unforgettable faces that will always be remembered: my fellow teachers, every single student, the street people, those wild and wooly backpackers, the crazy Rasta lady, beach kids, friends and lovers, and of course little Mimi. To each of you, I wish you great happiness.

When I started my teaching and traveling adventure I had no idea where it might lead. I just jumped in and did it. That's the way I do life. I wasn't looking for answers about myself, or going in search of a better life. I simply did it because it sounded fun and rewarding. I received an education beyond belief: of loving, caring, and giving from people who had nothing monetarily to give. Yet, they gave me the greatest gift of all, without wanting anything in return. They gave me their friendship, and often times their love.

I've experienced many journeys to some strange and magnificent places. Sometimes, they were difficult and stressful, and often a bit scary. However, more than half were so amazingly exquisite it made it all worthwhile. It was somewhat like giving birth, the difficulties turned into glorious beauty. My goal now is to carry these gifts I've received from around the world, and spread that beauty of the people I've met along my journey.

May all your travels be full of strange smells, interesting sights, beautiful new people, lonely at times, scary at times, even boring at times, but all leading to ---Your Own Great Adventure!